Extraordinary Stories

Good News from the Seasons of the Church

Published by: Don Pratt

Library of Congress Cataloging-in-Publications data is available on request.

ISBN-10: 0-578-28083-7

ISBN-13: 978-0-578-28083-7

First Edition, 2022

Extraordinary Stories

Good News From the Seasons of the Church

by

Don Pratt

Don Pratt, Palm Harbor, Florida

To Cindy, you have brought
untold joy to my story!

Table of Contents

Introduction

Our lives are one continuous story made up of many stories. This book has—in a sense—been many years in the making. It wasn't the writing that took that long, but recognizing the stories and their impact on my life took decades. I felt God leading me to become a pastor when I was a senior in high school. That road has led me through a decade of theological education and over three decades as a practicing pastor. (Yes, I'm still practicing with the hopes of getting it right one day!) My journey has taken me from Southern Baptists to the Cooperative Baptist Fellowship to the Florida Conference of the United Methodist Church, where I now serve as an Elder. If that trip sounds confusing and disjointed to you, you should have been in the driver's seat for it! I am grateful for the privilege I have been given to be a pastor to so many wonderful people over the years.

How does one know God's direction and purpose in their own life? How does one presume to stand before a crowd of people on Sunday morning and hope to have anything to say that might encourage or challenge them in their own faith? For me, the answers to those questions are found in the stories recorded in the Bible. Over the years, these stories have shaped, challenged, and changed me.

I believe that the stories in Scripture connect with our stories in more ways than most of us are aware. Fortunately, there are times in our lives when we can see the connection; we see how our story connects with God's story. The saints and mystics down through the years have been those who were able to point out those divine intersections.

I grew up in a tradition that did not practice liturgy or follow the Christian year. When I arrived at seminary, I discovered what I had missed. Since then, following the Christian calendar and using liturgy in worship have become meaningful standards in my life, to the point that I thought it important to arrange these stories according to the Christian year. For my friends who are already used to following the Christian Year, this will make perfect sense. Those friends for whom the Christian calendar is new will discover a refreshing way to measure the time in one trip around the sun.

The Christian Calendar begins with Advent, usually the last Sunday of November or the first Sunday of December. It is a time of anticipation and preparation. It is filled with stories of people who were waiting. Sometimes they were waiting with hope and joy. Sometimes they were in pain, waiting for relief. We all have our stories of waiting. We find hope and encouragement where our stories and theirs intersect, no matter how long we have been waiting.

Advent is followed by the season of Christmas. It lasts twelve days (like the song.) Christmas is the celebration that Christ is born! It is a time of reflecting on the unexpected actions of God in our world and in our own lives as well.

The next season is called ordinary time, and it begins with January 6th, Epiphany, or—as some call it—Kings Day. It is the day we celebrate that the Kings or Magi saw and worshipped the infant Jesus. Since these men were not Jewish, the emphasis is on how God's gift came not just to the Jewish community but to all of us Gentiles as well. It is a time to focus on the incarnation. God refused to stay away up in heaven but came down to where we are and got all into our business. When God was stuck away up in heaven, we could pretend that God was like whatever we wanted God to be like. God wasn't around to argue with us. But, the incarnation changed all of that. Now we know what God is like; God is like Jesus. We can no longer pretend that God agrees with our theology when Jesus clearly said and did things that do not. The Bible is full of stories of people trying to figure out how to deal with that, very much like our own stories of trying to figure out how to deal with Jesus. This season of ordinary time lasts until Ash Wednesday, which is the beginning of Lent.

The season of Lent is a time of reflection and repentance. During Lent, we remember the passion of Jesus. We steel ourselves to look at his suffering and death. It is not a time to wallow in morbid, mental self-flagellation. Instead, we are reminded that the story of Jesus is one of suffering as well as joy, of death as well as resurrection. This is where Jesus' story intersects with ours when we are going through hard times. We learn that God doesn't protect us from suffering but suffers with us. We face the fact that some of our suffering has been brought on by our own choices. We face that truth and turn from our old ways of doing things. We find that we are not suffering because God abandoned us. But, that, God is here with us, suffering beside us.

Easter is a season, not a day. One could argue that it is a way of life. All of the established institutions, political and religious, opposed Jesus and his teaching. He was not in line with the way they wanted life to work. So, they killed him. It was their way of saying that they were right and Jesus was wrong about God and life and how the world should work. The resurrection was God's way of saying, "Not so fast!" The resurrection is God's "Yes" to Jesus' life and teaching and God's "No" to the established way of doing things. It still is. Those who live in the light of the resurrection have discovered a way to life, peace, justice, and joy that comes from following Jesus' way of life. Not all of the powers in Heaven and Earth can overcome it. They have often tried and often failed. The resurrection is not a past event but a present reality. We live with hope because Jesus is alive and with us now, today.

Easter lasts for fifty days and is followed by Pentecost. Pentecost is the day we celebrate the gift of the Holy Spirit. Fifty days after the resurrection, the Spirit of God showed up and breathed new life and power into a room full of disciples who then went out and changed the world. We understand Pentecost every time we recognize that God has breathed life back into us after our defeats and failures.

The time from Pentecost back to Advent is also called ordinary time. After years of reading and studying the Bible and following the Christian calendar, I have decided that ordinary time is a poor designation. When we are alive to our own stories and the story of God in our lives the times become extraordinary.

The Christian year covers the ebbs and flows of not only Jesus' life, but of ours as well. We may not experience things on the same timetable, but we experience them, nonetheless. Throughout the year, we will experience anticipation, purpose, shadows or difficult times, joy, and surprise in the midst of everyday living.

If you are not sure about this whole religion or God thing, these stories are for you. They are stories about doubt and confusion. They are stores of struggle and a sincere search for the truth. You may find yourself in more of these stories than you would imagine. Following Jesus does not mean that you have no doubts. It just means you have discovered a strength and love that keeps you going even in your doubts.

Christians will find these old stories told in a fresh new way. You will find them as relevant today as when they were first told. You will also find yourself in these stories. They are stories of sinners and saints. As followers of Jesus, we are both living in the constant tension of our story of being a sinner and a saint.

If you are tasked with preaching these stories to a local congregation, I hope you will find some insight and direction in these stories. All the stories can be found in the lectionary and are told in order of the Christian Year. I hope they will be a resource for your own thinking and retelling of these stories.

I hope that in the reading of these extraordinary stories you will realize that the God who created everything that exists loves you, and your life is an Extraordinary Story.

Living In Expectation

We spend a lot of our lives in expectation.

Waiting.

Preparing.

It seems that much of life is lived waiting for the next part of life to get started. Children can't wait to be teenagers. Teenagers can't wait to be "adults." High Schoolers can't wait to get to college. College students can't wait to get a job. On and on and on it goes. Then at some point, you start looking back instead of forward, either with celebration or regret or some of both.

The Bible is full of stories of people living in expectation. The most pronounced of these are the stories of Advent. God promised for a long time that a Messiah would come. People were living in times of difficulty and discouragement with hopeful anticipation of the fulfillment of God's promise.

Think of all the times you have lived in expectation of something. Now listen to their stories, stories of anticipation and hopeful waiting. Allow their stories of expectation to guide you in your times of expectation.

§

Mary's Song (Luke 1:47-55)

I am going to admit to you that I like musical theater. From *Oklahoma* and *South Pacific* to *Mary Poppins* and *The Sound of Music* to *The Phantom of the Opera*, *Les Misérables*, *Wicked* and *Hamilton*, I love a good musical.

It seems strange to some people to be watching a play or movie and right in the middle of a scene, someone just breaks out into song. That rarely happens in real life. As a matter of fact, church is one of the few places left where there is public singing in the United States anyway. At concerts, most of the time, it's just the professionals singing. At Karaoke night at the local pub, a lot of people wish only the professionals were allowed to sing!

But, there is something great about musicals. My favorite musical is Fiddler On The Roof. I fell in love with the story and the music as a teenager. I have loved it ever since. And, on occasion, I do find myself humming, "If I were a rich man."

This has nothing to do with the story, but I want you to have appropriate sympathy for my now-adult children. To wake them when they were in school, I used to stand in the hallway by the doors of their rooms and sing, in Italian, an aria I learned in college. They assured me they were the only kids in their class who had been awaked by an Italian aria for school. It is not just me either. Other members of my family do occasionally break out into song for no apparent reason.

I am going to ask you to think of the birth narratives in the Gospel of Luke as a musical. There are four texts in the first two chapters that are referred to as "songs." The songs even have names; The Magnificat or Mary's Song, The Benedictus or Zechariah's Song, The Gloria or the Angel's Song, The Nunc Dimittis or Simeon's Song.

Let's listen to the lead number in the first musical in Luke. Right in the middle of the narrative, Mary breaks into song.

The song is called "The Magnificat." The name comes from the first word of the song in the Latin translation, and the song consists mostly of direct quotes from the Hebrew Bible. (For those of you interested in this kind of thing, you should read 1 Samuel 2:1-10. You can see how closely Mary's Song follows Hannah's prayer.)

This is the story in the lectionary for the First Sunday of Advent. Advent is a time of preparation. It is a time for us to get ready for what it really means that Christ is born among us. I think Mary's song offers some clues that help us prepare for this Christmas event.

The prophets and the New Testament writers tell us the same thing: we cannot really experience the Christmas event unless we prepare ourselves for it.

We may not be fully prepared. The chances are we won't be. But we can be better prepared than we would have been. Take Mary, for example. She didn't understand all that this child was going to be and do. But, she prepared as best she could for what was going to happen to her.

Mary's story is such an important story. Unfortunately, it has been over sentimentalized. We probably don't understand the story as well as we think we do. Mary was but a child herself. She was most likely somewhere between 12 and 14 years old. She had been shielded from most of the going's-on in the world around her.

She was engaged to a nice man, and everything was going along just as it should when an angel appeared to her. The angel told her that she was going to have a baby and that child would be the Son of God. Against all odds, Mary believed it. She believed, even if she did not fully understand all the ways her world was going to change.

Later, after Jesus' birth, Mary would be warned by an old man in the Temple. His name was Simeon, and part of his song went like this:

This child is destined to cause the falling and rising of many in Israel, and to be a sign that will be spoken against—and a sword will pierce your own soul too.

What could he possibly mean? How could this child cause Mary any sorrow, especially sorrow like that of a sword piercing her own soul? Mary could not even imagine that there could be anything like a cross in this child's future. She wasn't prepared for that. She was prepared for the fact that he would enter this world covered in her blood. She was not prepared for the fact that when he left this world she would be covered in his blood. She had no way of knowing.

Nor was Mary prepared for what was going to happen that night she rode into Bethlehem on the back of a donkey. This is important for us to understand: Mary didn't know or understand everything that was going to happen. She didn't know what Jesus was going to be or do. The angel asked her to just be prepared for his birth. So, she did. Then she took one step at a time, day after day, learning just who this child really was.

It is the same for you and me as we prepare for Christmas. We don't know everything that it means that God became flesh and blood and lived among us. The theological word for that is "incarnation." We don't know all that it will mean for us to follow him. So, like Mary, we prepare for what we do know. We follow one step at a time, one day at a time.

After Mary received her good news from the angel, she visited her cousin, Elizabeth. Elizabeth was also expecting. Her child would grow up to be the wild and wooly John the Baptist. When Mary first greeted Elizabeth, Elizabeth's baby leaped inside her. Elizabeth blessed Mary and called her "the mother of my Lord."

Then—as only happens in musicals and in Luke's Gospel—Mary broke into song. "My soul glorifies the Lord." It is a song of praise. Praise for what God had done for her. She thanked God for choosing her. She understood that there were others out there who were older, wiser, wealthier—the list goes on. But God chose her. She thanked God for choosing her.

Then she thanked God for his goodness to everyone. God did not just show mercy to Mary. God shows and has shown mercy to people for generations.

Maybe this is the first step of preparation for us as well: to begin with praise. Maybe that is how we need to begin this Advent Season. It may be health you praise God for, or family or friends or material blessings, or—perhaps most important— for allowing you to be a part of God's family and God's purpose. The commercials entice us to begin this season thinking of the things we don't have and need to buy. But, the truth is, we are better prepared when we praise God for what we do have, the things that we can't buy. The first step in preparation is praise.

In her song, Mary sings of how the rulers are brought down and the lowly are lifted up. The rich have things taken away and the poor have things given to them. In other words, God evens the playing field. The "Haves" have less, and the "Have-nots" have more. In the Kingdom of God there are no inequities of wealth, or of power, or of grace. God's grace levels the field, so that when we see others, we do not see them as more or less valuable than us; we understand that we are all equal in worth and value.

This understanding is an important step of preparation too. We tend to judge people by what they have or don't have, by what they do, instead of who they are. At family Christmas gatherings we try to impress each other with what we have accomplished. At office parties we try to hang out in the "right" circles. We want to impress certain people.

We will not understand this season until we see everyone as a person of value to God. The Messiah who came chose to be born to a poor young couple, not a King or Queen. He chose to be born in a barn, not a palace, and he was first greeted by shepherds, not dignitaries. Surely, he would have a hard time understanding our differentiating between rich and poor, powerful and weak, skin color, and country of origin. No one that you meet this season is more or less valuable to God than you are. Everyone you meet this season is a person that God loves.

The last verse in Mary's song says that God *"has helped his servant Israel, remembering to be merciful."*

Remembering to be merciful. I like that phrase. God remembered to be merciful to Israel. God led them out of slavery in Egypt, and in the end, they did not remain faithful to God. But God remembered to be merciful to them.

People in Mary's day were living under Roman oppression longing for the day when God would hear their prayers and send the long-awaited Messiah. God remembered to be merciful to them.

We attempt to follow God, and then we mess up. Our best intentions often fall short. But then, God remembers to be merciful to us.

Too often, this Advent/Christmas Season turns into a hurried, helter-skelter time. By now, our cultural consumerism is in high gear. It seems to start earlier every year. It started weeks before Advent. Someone went to a store right after Halloween, and the store was already decorated and pushing presents for Christmas. The person said, "They were already all decked out for Christmas, and Mary hasn't even told Joseph yet!"

Mary finishes her song. The orchestra music comes to an end. Mary hangs out with Elizabeth for three more months and then heads home. Here is what I take away from Mary and her song.

We will never be fully prepared for what God wants to do in our lives in the future. We prepare for what we know now and put one foot in front of the other, moving in the direction God leads us. Be faithful in what we do know.

Give God praise for all the good things in your life. Don't enter this season worrying about what you don't have. Look around and be grateful for what you do have.

Don't feel inferior or superior to others. Just love the people around you. We all have equal worth and value before God.

Don't forget that God always remembers us with mercy. It could be that this Christmas some folks are too busy mourning their past to enjoy their present or celebrate their future. God remembers us in mercy. God's mercy is greater than our sin.

Maybe if we do these things we will be better prepared this year for the birth of Jesus. That's what the song says.

§

Zach's Song (Luke 1:68-79)

Names are interesting. I enjoy hearing stories of how people got their names or why they gave their children certain names. In fact, the story of how I got my name is pretty unusual.

I come from a large family. I'm the youngest of ten kids. By the time I came along, my mom had apparently run out of names and energy. Someone asked, "What are you going to name him?" My mom and dad didn't say anything. So, my oldest sister named me.

My Dad was 56 years old when I was born, and I think he was mostly just in shock. Like Zechariah, in this story, my dad just sat there in silence and stared at the wall, occasionally shaking his head. Finally, my sister piped up with a name, and my mom said, "Sure." So, here I am. I consider myself fortunate. My name could have been so much worse if I'd been named by some of my other brothers or sisters. It could have been bad.

In the Bible, and in most families, names are usually chosen with greater care than mine. In the Bible, names are significant, and here the names are important to the story.

First, let me tell you the part of the story that happened earlier. Zechariah was a priest. Both he and his wife Elizabeth loved God and were faithful followers. One day it was his turn to go into the Temple and do some priestly stuff. While he was there, the angel, Gabriel, appeared to him. At first, Zechariah was afraid. The angel told Zechariah and Elizabeth that they were going to have a son. This boy of theirs would play a special role in helping prepare the way for the Messiah. The boy's name was to be John.

Zechariah and Elizabeth were both on up in years, and Zechariah did not believe Gabriel. It sounded too good to be true. Zechariah probably laughed and said, "Okay, where is the hidden camera? Is it over there behind that Cherubim?" He didn't believe it, so he asked Gabriel for a sign to prove he was for real. Gabriel said, "Here is your sign!" He told Zechariah that he would not be able to speak until the day these things came true. The moral of the story is, "don't ask angels for signs."

When Zechariah came out of the Temple he could not speak. Everyone knew he must have seen some kind of vision. When his time of service at the Temple was over, he went home, and sure enough, just as the angel had said, his wife Elizabeth became pregnant.

It was customary to name male children on the eighth day at the circumcision ceremony. The angel Gabriel told Zechariah he would not be able to speak until the things he had foretold came true. The last two prophecies were fulfilled at his ceremony.[1]

Gabriel had predicted that many people would rejoice at the birth of this child. Everyone was rejoicing.

Gabriel had said that this child would be named John. As soon as Zechariah and Elizabeth made it official that his name was John, Zechariah could speak again. Actually, it says that to communicate to Zachariah they were making signs to him, which seems to indicate that not only could Zechariah not speak, but he couldn't hear either. But, when the child was named John, Zechariah was healed.

Imagine witnessing all of the events that surrounded John's birth. The miracle of his mother, Elizabeth, delivering him on her Medicare policy. His father, Zechariah, seeing an angel and being unable to speak and evidently unable to hear. Then, when John was named, Zechariah was miraculously healed, just as the angel said he would be. Everyone knew this was not an ordinary birth. So, this could not be an ordinary child. They wondered, *"What is this child going to be?"*

---

[1] *Raymond Brown, The Birth of The Messiah, p.375.*

It is in response to this question that Zechariah breaks into song. His song is, in part, an answer to the question, *"What is this child going to be?"*

Because of these miracles surrounding John's birth, there were many people who believed that John must be the Messiah. And later on in John's life, there would be people who would be confused about who John was. So, from the very beginning, at John's birth, the Holy Spirit speaks (or sings) through Zechariah to tell us that John is not the Messiah. The focus of the story will be Jesus, not John.

I want to take a moment here to address an issue that is lightly addressed in this story; "That is, persons whose work it is to point others to Jesus can themselves become objects and centers of the affection and loyalty of many."[2]

John ended up with a lot of disciples. In the Gospels, we encounter stories that tell of some of the confusion between Jesus' disciples and John's disciples. At times, there was even some competition between them. Later, in the Book of Acts, which was also written by Luke, we find people like Apollos, who appears to have been a disciple of John.

This kind of mix-up still happens today. People become followers of pastors or church staff instead of followers of Jesus. Sometimes it happens innocently, but sometimes pastors encourage it. Pastors have this sacred honor of being invited into people's lives during times of sorrow and of joy. Bonds form, and there is nothing wrong with that. But, sometimes, we let it go too far. Some people allow the messenger to take the place of the message in their lives. Everyone loves to be appreciated. But, good messengers keep the focus on the message, not themselves. The message is Jesus.

Here, at the very beginning of John's life, we are reminded that it is about Jesus. John will be a great man. Jesus said there was none greater in the kingdom of God than John. That is a pretty good reference for your resume right there! God will use John in great ways.

[2] Fred Craddock, *"Luke"*, Interpretation Commentary, p.32.

But it is not about John. It is about Jesus. It is John's own father who reminds us of that truth. It is about Jesus, not us.

So, after the people wonder out loud who John would become, you hear the music start, and Zechariah moves to center stage and begins to sing. Theologians refer to his song as the Benedictus. Again, the title is from the first word of this passage in the Latin translation. I call it Zach's song.

Like Mary's Song, Zach's Song begins with praise. Praise for the Messiah who is on his way. Praise for the Messiah who brings all of us back to God and will make us whole. He uses a really interesting picture. He says the Messiah is like a "horn of salvation."[3] Imagine an animal like a bull. If he charges you and connects his horns with you, you will feel the full strength and force of the bull through his horns. Or, maybe a rhino is a better example because he only has one horn. If he catches you with his one horn, you will feel all of his strength and power concentrated in that horn. Jesus is like that horn. In his incarnation, his life, his cross, his death, and his resurrection, God concentrated all of the power of our salvation. God's forgiveness and mercy were directed towards us in the event of the life of Jesus. It is through Jesus that we find forgiveness and mercy and life.

It's.

About.

Jesus.

After that, there is a short instrumental riff followed by verse two, which is about John. John is not the Messiah, but he is the one who will prepare the way for the Messiah. That will be his job. And that is what John did. He went ahead, pointing the way to Jesus as the One God sent to lead us back into a relationship with God. John was important, and he played an important role in God's plan. But, it wasn't about John.

It's.

---

[3] Norval Geldenhuys, "Luke", NICNT, p.93.

About.

Jesus.

One of the best things we can do to prepare for Christmas is to remember that is it about Jesus.

It's.

About.

Jesus.

There are so many things this time of year that distract us. Mostly they are not bad things. They are good things: presents to buy, food to prepare, parties or gatherings to go to, or maybe even host, a house to decorate.

Sometimes we get a little selfish. We want things to go a certain way or work out a certain way, and we don't get our way. All of the kids don't come home for Christmas. Not everyone is as appreciative as they should be. You didn't get the gift you had hoped for, or you couldn't afford to give the gift you wanted to give. It just wasn't the Christmas you wanted. And it's easy for us to get down or get upset.

I know of a person who complained to a friend that Christmas did not go the way he had wanted. It did not go according to his plans. His friend said to him, "Christmas is not *your* birthday." When it's your birthday, you can complain if everything doesn't go like you want, but it isn't your birthday. It's Jesus' birthday.

It's.

About.

Jesus.

There is a short bridge, and then the song ends with these words:

> . . . *because of the tender mercy of our God, by which the rising sun will come to us from heaven to shine on those living in darkness and in the shadow of death, to guide our feet into the path of peace.*

Zach's Song helps us get the focus back on Jesus. Jesus is the One who came to bring light to those who live in the darkness of confusion and doubt and sin. Jesus is the One who came to bring comfort to those who are walking or have just walked through the shadow of death. Jesus is the One who came to lead us out of our personal chaos and anxiety and into his peace. And he does it all, not with threats of judgment, but with tender mercy.

Some may have thought Zechariah just an old fool for jumping up and singing like that. But, you can't blame him, really. Not when you know what he knew. How could you not sing?

I think, in the end, Zach's Song is here to remind us that the best way to prepare for Christmas is to not get distracted. Don't get sidetracked. As impressive as the events around John's birth were, it was not about John.

It's.

About.

Jesus.

I love this season. I really do. It is my favorite time of the year. There will be gifts and parties and decorations and extra food. There will be memories made and relationships cherished. Enjoy them. Enjoy them all. Soak them all in. But don't get distracted. As great as the season is, as great as all of those things are, the greatest thing is Jesus. That's what Zechariah is telling us. It's about Jesus.

It's.

About.

Jesus.

§

Simeon's Song (Luke 2:22-38)

For many years, Dr. Clyde Fant was President of the International Baptist Seminary in Switzerland. One year while he was there, everyone gathered in the chapel for the children's Christmas pageant. It was like most other children's Christmas pageants you've seen except the children were from twenty-eight different nations.

They were dressed in their daddy's bathrobes playing the parts of wise men, shepherds, and angels. Everything was ready. The wise men were from Switzerland, Tanzania, and Yugoslavia. Shepherds were from Scotland, Germany, Brazil, and Denmark. Joseph was from Japan, and Mary was from Nigeria. They were all on the stage, and everyone was waiting. And waiting. The children begin to fidget nervously.

Finally, the lady in charge, who was seated at the piano, stood up and said, "Well, I'm sorry folks, we're just waiting on an angel." And in about thirty seconds, in came a tiny child still straightening her cardboard wings. Then the play began.[4]

We are not good at waiting. I heard about a woman whose car stalled while she was stopped at a traffic light. She tried and tried, but the car would not start. The light turned green, and a man in a car behind her began honking his horn. The light changed a few times. Her car wouldn't start. The man behind her kept honking his horn. Finally, she got out of her car and went back to the man behind her. He rolled down his window just a bit. She very politely told him that her car would not start, and she did not know how to get it to start.

---

[4] *Clyde Fant, "Waiting On An Angel" sermon delivered at Stetson University Chapel, Deland, FL on Nov. 30, 1988.*

But, if he thought he could get it to start, she would be happy to sit in his car and honk the horn for him while he worked on it.

We are not good at waiting. We are not a patient people. We are more of a car horn honking, Express lane, Amazon Prime shipping, in a hurry bunch of folks. No, we don't wait well at all.

Let me tell you a story about someone who was waiting. His name was Simeon. The story begins in the Temple in Jerusalem.

Mary and Joseph took their newborn son to the Temple to meet the requirements of the Law. The Law stated that every firstborn male had to be dedicated to God, complete with the sacrifice of a lamb. But, if you were poor, the law allowed you to sacrifice two doves or pigeons instead. Joseph and Mary brought the birds.

An interesting aside is that Luke's Gospel begins in the Temple and ends in the Temple. Luke also explains to us in the Book of Acts that the church began in the Temple area, the apostles observed the hours of Temple prayers. Paul, after his conversion, prayed in the Temple and was finally arrested at the Temple while completing rites of purification. It is Luke's way of telling us that Jesus never rejected the Temple. Instead, he was rejected by the religious status quo of his time.[5]

Mary and Joseph were minding their own business, walking through the outer court of the Temple. It is important that this incident occurred in the outer court where everyone could see it, even the Gentiles who may have come to worship the God of Israel. The birth narratives illustrate how God did everything in public view. Jesus was born in a stable. The shepherds and the wise men came there to see him. God is at work, out in the open, right in front of us. Unfortunately, we are not always looking. The end result is that we often miss what God is doing.

A man named Simeon ran up to them and asked to hold their son. I am sure, at first, they thought he was just like the other senior adults who came over to them at McDonald's and asked to see the

---

[5] Fred Craddock, "Luke", Interpretation, pp. 37-38.

baby. He would probably smile and then tell them about his grand-children, show them a picture or two or fifty, and then be on his way.

But, Simeon had something different in mind. He took this child in his arms, and he blessed him. He praised God for him. You see, Simeon had been waiting a long time for this child.

We don't know much about Simeon. We do know he was waiting on the Savior to arrive. We know that God had promised him that he would not die until he saw the Savior, the Savior that God had promised to bring light into the darkness of our world. Simeon had been praying, but he had been waiting too. I'll bet whenever a new, handsome, young Priest walked by, Simeon looked at him long and hard to see if he was the One. Each time he heard of a dynamic new Rabbi, he went to hear him, wanting to see if he was the One. It seems that he had been waiting a long time. He was probably getting tired of waiting. His arthritis was acting up again. His back hurt, and he wasn't getting any younger. Still, he waited. He was quite surprised when he saw this poor, young couple walking through the Temple court carrying a baby, and deep inside his heart, he knew this was the day for which he had been waiting. Of all the places to look, he had never thought to check the cradle role.

He ran, as best he could, till he reached them. He asked to hold the child. Once the baby was cradled in his arms, Simeon looked long-ingly into his face. This was the One. God with chubby cheeks. Who could have dreamed this was the One he had been waiting for, for so long?

In his joy, he blessed the baby. He blessed the parents. Anyone passing by probably was hit with a stray blessing. A lifetime of wait-ing had finally come to an end.

Still holding the baby, Simeon lifted his face toward heaven. (Cue the orchestra.) Simeon is about to sing.

Simeon's Song is the last of the songs in Luke's Gospel. In the program, it is called the Nunc Dimittis, again from the first few words of these verses in the Latin version. In English, it would be

"Now Let Depart." Simeon's Song is short, only a chorus, but it is succinctly powerful.

> *Sovereign Lord, as you have promised, you now dismiss your servant in peace. For my eyes have seen your salvation, which you have prepared in the sight of all people, a light for revelation to the Gentiles and the glory to your people Israel.*

In this short song, Simeon tells us that in this baby he has discovered everything he has been waiting for his whole life. Seeing Jesus had made his life complete.

He spoke of how this Jesus was not just the One he had been waiting on, not just the One the Jewish nation had been waiting on, but he is the One we have all been waiting on, even the ones who don't know it yet. He was here. For Simeon, the wait was over. And the wait was worth it.

After the song, he told them some other things, then he handed the child back. Mary and Joseph looked at each other, not quite knowing what to say. Simeon wiped his eyes with his sleeve, told them goodbye, and hobbled off. He had told them some exciting things, some frightening things, and some strange things. But, it was his face they would never forget. It was the face of hope, rewarded.

There was also an elderly woman named Anna who came and spoke over the child as well. But, she did not have a singing role, so we won't spend any time there. Musical Theater is harsh!

At first, the story of Simeon sounds a little strange. A senior adult singing over a baby he didn't even know, blessing and praying and crying right out in the middle of the Temple courts, right there in front of God and everybody. Waiting and waiting. Then, actually believing that all of his hopes had been fulfilled by a poor infant wrapped in a blanket. It does sound strange.

But then again, maybe not. The Bible says that he was a devout man. He had a relationship with God. He prayed often and was in tune with what God was doing. Even in his waiting, he was obedient to God. Even when he did not understand, he recognized what God was doing. He recognized this child was the One he had been waiting for.

There were a lot of people in the Temple courts that day. But they didn't notice this child. They were on their way to worship and passed right by this poor couple and their baby. They were waiting too, but they weren't paying attention. I don't think they knew for sure what they were waiting for. They just knew something was missing. I am sure they thought the answer would involve more than a baby born to a peasant couple, too poor to afford a decent sacrifice.

Maybe that's not so strange at all. The scene is repeated, year after year. It is being repeated right now. A woman shops in the mall. She looks for just the right gift. But, what do you buy the man you have been married to for thirty years, who hardly notices you are alive? What gift can rekindle the flame? She looks and waits, hoping she can find the right present that will help start to change things.

A man dreads his first Christmas without his wife. He hopes something will come on Christmas Day and fill the emptiness inside. He waits. He hopes.

A gift is bought for a friend. Last year the gift was wrapped with excitement. But things have changed. Things were said this year that can't be taken back. This gift is wrapped with the hope that it will be accepted and a relationship can be put back on track. Wrap the gift and wait.

What do you buy the man who has everything and is still paying for it at 19% interest? Every year he feels a little emptier than he did the year before. He has always thought that by the time he made this much money and had all of these things, his life would be great. But he is still waiting, still hoping maybe this year things will be different.

Waiting. We all waiting for something. Many aren't quite sure what they are waiting for: they just know that something is missing. For many, whatever is missing becomes more noticeable this time of year. We should know better by now, but we keep thinking that it will come somewhere in the season itself. Somewhere in the carols and decorations and presents and gatherings that missing piece will come. But it never does.

We brush right past the poor couple with the baby. Surely, what we are waiting for has nothing to do with them. On that day in the Temple court, only Simeon understood the truth. And there are some who find it today. The truth is that son of that poor couple has everything to do with what we are waiting for.

Deep down inside, there is a longing that cannot be filled by presents. We won't find it at the next party. Deep down, we know that what we are waiting for is to be loved, to be accepted, to be forgiven. We are waiting for a love big enough to embrace us. We are waiting for a love big enough to change us. We are waiting for a love big enough to transform our lives and make us new. What we are waiting for is a Savior.

The Good News that Simeon is singing about is that our Savior is here. He didn't come as we expected. But he came. He brought with him the fulfillment of our greatest hopes and needs. He brought with him all of the things we have been waiting for to make our lives new. What we have been waiting for is a Savior.

This Christmas, I hope you realize the waiting is over. Christmas is about giving thanks that the waiting is over. The Savior has come. Put down the presents and eggnog and approach the poor couple. Look inside the blanket at this baby young Mary holds in her arms. God became flesh and lives among us. God lives among us because he loves you. We have been waiting for God to live among us and be at work in our lives. REJOICE! God has heard our prayer.

Preparing For Christmas (Matthew 3:1-12)

Has anyone asked you this question yet? "Are you ready for Christmas?" If not, someone probably will before the season is over. We all know Christmas doesn't just happen. It takes preparation. There is a list of things we have to do to prepare for Christmas.

We have to go and get a tree. For some of you, that is a trip to Lowe's or a Christmas tree lot. For some of you, it is a trip to the closet or garage. But, where ever we get the tree, we set it up and put the lights and ornaments on it.

One year we had a nice big Christmas tree that the cat, for some reason, loved to climb. The problem was when he climbed it, he ended up knocking it over. Several times. Fortunately, the tree made it till Christmas. And miraculously, so did the cat.

Usually, there is some extra cooking involved. Holiday meals, holiday cookies and treats. At our house it is Baklava. We get Baklava on the high holy days of Christmas and Easter.

We decorate the house. Some people have all kinds of inside decorations that just put you in the spirit of the holiday. Many folks spend a great deal of effort decorating the outside. They put up enough Christmas lights to rival the Griswold family. And now, there are those big blow-up lawn decorations to add to the festivities.

Almost everyone makes more of an effort to be a little nicer this time of year. Show people a little more grace.

Even children prepare. They plot and they plan how to get the gifts they really want. I heard about a little boy who wanted a puppy for Christmas. His best friend got a puppy for Christmas the year before, so he asked him, "How did you get your parents to give you a puppy for Christmas?" His friend told him that he asked his parents for a little brother. They gave him a puppy.

Christmas after Christmas, we do the same things, and we prepare the same way each year. And yet, something still seems to be missing. Could there be something missing from our preparation? Could it be that there is more to preparing for Christmas than fruitcakes and exterior illumination? Could there be something else we need to consider as we prepare for Christmas?

Christmas is about Christ coming to be with us. Advent is our time of preparing for that event. In the New Testament, there was a man named John who tried to help people prepare.

John the Baptist. He wasn't really a Baptist. There were no Baptists back then. Baptists didn't show up until the 17th century. A better translation would be John the baptizer, so-called because of his custom of baptizing people. Although converts to Judaism were baptized, John's purpose for baptism was unusual to them.

The prophets said that one like Elijah must come before the Messiah. Jesus later said that John was that person. Some things about John recalled Elijah. Both of them "appeared out of the desert." They even dressed alike. They both wore a garment of hair with a belt around it.

I like the way Fred Craddock describes John. "He was no beautiful candle burning in the sanctuary. He was a prairie fire, the very fire of God scorching the earth."[6]

Like Elijah, John showed up out of the desert in his camel hair coat and leather belt. It probably had his initials, J.B., etched on the back. His message was one of preparation. But, it wasn't "decorate the house" or "get the tree." It wasn't "hang the stockings." His message of preparation was, "REPENT!"

What! The Christmas messages we are used to hearing are messages of peace and hope and goodwill toward all people. It is warm and fuzzy and feel good. Repent! Where did he come up with that?

---

[6] Fred Craddock, *The Collected Sermons of Fred B. Craddock*, p.111.

Maybe he was a Baptist! I think this is why John is not usually included in the Christmas story. But, the lectionary includes at least one reading about John every year during Advent. Preparing the way for the Messiah is an important part of preparing for Christmas. But, John doesn't fit our themes very well.

That is why there are no Christmas cards with John the Baptist on them. I have looked. They don't make them. So, I made one. A John the Baptist Christmas card. On the front is a picture of John the Baptist with the word, "Repent!" You open it up, and on the inside, it says, "Our thoughts for you at this special time of the year are best expressed by the one who said, "You pack of snakes! Who told you to flee from the wrath to come? Merry Christmas."

These would be great for relatives. Some of you are thinking, "I know some folks I would like to send that to." John the Baptist Christmas cards. Probably an idea whose time has come.

Repent, though. That word has such a negative connotation in our minds. When you hear the word, it is almost impossible not to envision some large, angry preacher with his hair swooshed back, red-faced, telling us that if we don't repent, we will burn in hell. Sometimes we see someone holding up a sign with just that one word on it. Repent. We recoil from it a little.

Maybe it is time we reclaimed the word "Repent." The word simply means "Change." Change. It doesn't mean, "feel bad about something you have done." It doesn't mean that you should feel bad about who you are." It doesn't mean, "I'll try to be a better person." No, repent means I am going to change, starting right now. I am going to think differently. I am going to live differently.

That is the message John was trying to get us to understand all along. The Messiah is coming. We will all have to change. When Jesus gets here and initiates his kingdom, things cannot just rock along as usual. Things will have to change. We have to change because God's kingdom doesn't operate on the same rules and values as our culture. We can't live in God's kingdom thinking and acting the same way we live now. When the Messiah gets here, things are going to change. So, get ready.

Some people welcomed this news because they were ready for a change. Those who were disenfranchised by the current system welcomed a new way of doing things.

Of course, there were those who were not so happy about change. That is how it always works. If the system works for you, then you don't want to change it. If it doesn't work for you, then you are more open to change. The system was working great for the political and religious professionals, so they weren't too happy about all of John's talk about change. They felt threatened by it.

"Change!" shouted the old baptizer. "Christ is here among us. We prepare by changing."

In our current system, consumerism is a god we worship, and Christmas is a hyped-up version of that. Your worth is determined by how much you own and how much it cost. Your love for your family is measured by how much you spend on Christmas gifts. Those who profit from this system don't want you to change. They want you to keep buying into the system and buying their stuff. No wonder some of them don't like Jesus.

In Jesus' kingdom, the only good reason for having more money than you need is to give it away to help others. Your worth is determined by the fact that you were created in the image of God. Nothing else. And your love for your family is determined by your actions toward them, not what you can afford to give them.

Jesus' kingdom and the current kingdom are at odds. They are clashing. You want to be ready for Jesus' kingdom? You will have to change. So will I.

Another god in our current kingdom is tribalism. We are told to love the people like us. The ones who look like us, think like us, vote like us. Because we are American, or white, or male, or fill-in-the-blank, we are somehow better than others.

In Jesus' kingdom we don't think like that. In Jesus' kingdom all people are valued. All people have worth. We love all people the same.

Jesus' kingdom and the current kingdom are at odds. They are clashing. You want to be ready for Jesus' kingdom? You will have to change. So will I.

In the current kingdom, it is "me first." "Us first." "Our country first." After I have taken care of myself, then I will think about others. Me first, neighbor next, if at all.

In Jesus' kingdom, others come first. Their needs come before our needs. The night before he was murdered, Dr. Martin Luther King, Jr. preached a sermon on the parable of the Good Samaritan. He said this about the Levite and the Samaritan when they saw the man beaten and lying in a ditch:

> The first question that the Levite asked was, 'If I stop to help this man, what will happen to me?'" But when the Good Samaritan came by, he reversed the question and asked, "If I do not stop and help this man, what will happen to him?[7]

In this kingdom, we ask, "But what will happen to me if I put others first?" In Jesus' kingdom, we ask, "If I don't put others first, what will happen to them?" You want to be ready for Jesus' kingdom? You will have to change. So will I.

The great temptation is to just keep living by the rules of our present kingdom and just pretend it's Christian. A lot of people do that. Just keep doing what is best for me and claim that is what Jesus is about. But that is a lie.

Or, if we believe John the baptizer, we change. We start living by the values of Jesus' kingdom here and now, even though they will clash with the values of the present kingdom. And those who benefit

---

[7] *Dr. Martin Luther King, Jr. quoted by Jim Wallis, Christ in Crisis, p.25.*

from the present system will not like the changes or the change agents. Sometimes those who benefit from the present system include us. That is the real reason we don't want to change. That is why it is so hard.

It's no wonder there are no John the Baptist Christmas Cards or a John the Baptist figurine to put in the manger scene in our creche. He had the unenviable task of trying to help us to prepare for the one who is coming. The one whose kingdom is not at all like the kingdoms and empires we are used to, those that we benefit from now.

But, people came. They came from all over. And they asked John, "How can I prepare for the coming of Jesus and his kingdom?"

And John grabbed them by the neck and pushed them down into the muddy Jordan. They came up spitting and coughing, and John said, "Merry Christmas! The Times They Are A-Changin! If you want to be prepared for Jesus and his kingdom, you will have to change."

That was God's message to them. And that is God's message to us. How do we prepare for Christmas?

By the grace of God, we change. We start living by the law of love of Jesus' kingdom instead of the laws of our current culture. You will have to change. So will I.

§

Living With Purpose

It is great when you have purpose and direction in your life. All of us have gone through times when we have felt like we were spinning our wheels, stuck in a time of expectation. Then there are those times when we have seized a purpose or direction, or more accurately, a purpose or direction has seized us. We live with more confidence. Life seems to be more fulfilling.

Hear these stories of people who lived with purpose. They had a direction and a reason to get up each morning. They lived in a way that all of us might wish to live every day. May their stories of purpose inspire you to pursue the things you are passionate about, the things that really matter, and may they make it exciting for you to get up each day.

§

Jonah: God's Great Comedy (The Book of Jonah)

A lot of people don't realize it, but the Book of Jonah is a comedy. It has a serious theme, as many comedies do. But it is a comedy. So, forget all the debates about the fish and just listen again to the story. Feel free to laugh. I will include certain verses of Scripture along the way just so you know I am not making this up!

It all starts when Jonah gets an unwanted transfer.

> *The Word of the LORD came to Jonah, son of Amittai: "Go to the great city of Nineveh and preach against it because its wickedness has come up before me.*

Nineveh, Shmineveh! Jonah hated Nineveh. He hated the people who lived there. He had no intention of going there, especially to warn them that the wrath of God was headed their way. He wanted God to destroy them. He would buy a ticket to watch that!

Now, before you get the idea that Jonah is just some small-minded prophet who was tired of hearing Ninevites talk about the way they did things up north, there were some reasons most Israelites hated Ninevites. Nineveh was an Assyrian city. Israel and the Assyrians had been at war. The Assyrians were known for their violence and cruelty. When they invaded Israel, they paid no attention to the Geneva Convention. In the name of war, the Assyrians did terrible, unspeakable things to the Israelites, and the Israelites did not forget.

So, when God said, "Jonah, Go to the Ninevites." Jonah said, "Not me." "No way, Yahweh!"[8] Then Jonah went to Joppa and got on a ship going in the opposite direction.

---

[8] *Stephen Shoemaker, "Jonah," Retelling the Biblical Story, p.92.*

Jonah discovered that it is hard to run from God. A storm came up. The ship was tossed about. Even the seasoned sailors were getting scared. But Jonah was asleep in his berth. This part of the story really frustrates me. I think of all the nights I have stayed up worrying about whether or not I have made the right decision. And there is Jonah; he knows he is doing the opposite of what God wants him to do, and he sleeps like a baby. The sailors had to wake him up and tell him to start praying because it looked like they might all drown.

In the midst of a crisis, the most important thing to do is find someone to blame! So, they all threw dice to determine whose fault it was that this storm was upon them. The numbers pointed to Jonah, so they made him "fess up." Jonah said, "I am a Hebrew. I fear the God who created all things and who is in control of all things (including these dice!)." Jonah told them to just go ahead and throw him overboard, and the storm would stop. The sailors didn't want to do that. They tried everything they could think of to no avail. Finally, they threw Jonah over. Jonah didn't seem to mind. He actually preferred drowning to going to Nineveh.

As soon as Jonah hit the water, the storm stopped. As he disappeared beneath the waves, a huge fish swallowed him. The sailors were stunned; Jonah was stunned. And I can't help but think the fish was stunned as well.

While getting the first submarine ride to Nineveh inside the fish, Jonah had some time to think and pray. After three days, the fish spit Jonah out on the beach. At least two prayers were answered that day. The prayer of Jonah and the prayer of the fish.

> Then the Word of the LORD came to Jonah a second time: Go to the great city of Nineveh and proclaim to it the message I give you. Jonah obeyed the word of the LORD and went to Nineveh. Now Nineveh was a very large city; it took three days to go through it.

Déjà vu. God gave Jonah a second chance. This time Jonah did what he was told. But, notice Jonah's attitude had not changed much.

Jonah just figured after running away and getting caught in a storm at sea, thrown overboard, swallowed by a fish, then spit up on the shore at Nineveh, that he didn't have much choice. So, Jonah went and warned them about the wrath of God to come, the whole time hoping they would not listen and would be destroyed. You can imagine, it must have been a really heartwarming sermon that Jonah preached. Stephen Shoemaker paraphrased it like this; it had three points,

1) God is just,
2) You are sinners,
3) Buh bye.

But, something incredible happened. As it often happens, in spite of the preacher, God got his message across. The people of Nineveh repented. They turned to God and asked God for forgiveness. And God forgave them. The people rejoiced, God laughed, and Jonah stomped away to sulk.

> *"But to Jonah this seemed very wrong, and he became angry. He prayed to the LORD, "Isn't this what I said, LORD, when I was still at home? That is what I tried to forestall by fleeing to Tarshish. I knew that you are a gracious and compassionate God, slow to anger and abounding in love, a God who relents from sending calamity."*

Jonah was hot! "I knew you would do this, God! I don't like these people! And you, you just forgive them. You are too soft on people. There are rules! I know we are supposed to love everybody, but I am telling you, God, that doesn't work in the real world. You just don't understand."

God tried to talk to Jonah about his anger management skills, but Jonah just stormed away again. Jonah went up on top of a hill, made himself a little shelter from the Sun, and sat down. He was watching to see what would happen to Nineveh. He was hoping and praying for at least a little fire and brimstone. Surely everyone had not repented.

God couldn't resist. God caused a plant to grow up over Jonah and provide shade from the heat. Jonah liked that. Then a worm entered the plant, and the plant died. And God turned up the heat a little bit. Jonah was angry again. And again, God asked Jonah why he was so angry? Jonah said he was angry because God had let that little plant die, and Jonah liked that little plant.

The story and the book end with God saying to Jonah;

> *"But the LORD said, "You have been concerned about this plant, though you did not tend it or make it grow. It sprang up overnight and died overnight. And should I not have concern for the great city of Nineveh, in which there are more than a hundred and twenty thousand people who cannot tell their right hand from their left – and also many animals?"*

The story leaves us with a lot of questions. Does Jonah ever repent? Does Jonah ever learn to love the Ninevites? How is Jonah going to explain the part about the fish to his friends or twenty-first-century literalists? But, these questions aren't really important. The story is not about Jonah. It is not about the fish. The story is about God.

For one thing, it is a story about how God can use stubborn, self-willed, salty people if they will just listen and be obedient. That is certainly good news. Good news for all of us. It is our only hope.

But, it is, first and foremost, a story about drawing circles. We are all circle drawers. Jonah was a circle drawer. We draw circles around the people and places that we think God loves. And we inevitably leave people outside of those circles. Jonah drew a circle around Israel. He drew a circle around people like him and left the Ninevites outside. The story shows Jonah—and us—that God draws bigger circles than we do. God's included the Ninevites.

Most of us need to draw bigger circles. Like Jonah, we want to draw geographical circles. Many want to draw a circle around the United States. But, we are all in this together. God created every human being on this planet in God's image. God loves us all the same. The pandemic should have taught us that what happens to someone in China or Korea or Italy affects us all. The world has gotten smaller. We are all in this thing together. The wider we draw our circle, the more people we care about, not less, the better off we all are.

During the Covid pandemic, there were actually politicians and some billionaires debating drawing a circle around the economy and capitalism and leaving the most vulnerable outside of that circle. Full disclosure, I'm not a politician or a billionaire, but I am a Christian. I am a human being, and I know that every person is created in the image of God. The rich and the poor. God has always drawn a circle around the most vulnerable among us. It is against everything Jesus lived and against the very character of God to even consider putting money above people. Jesus even said, "You can't serve money and God." And if you have to choose, remember, God always chooses people.

We are all guilty. We want to draw our circles around the people like us, who live where we live and think like we think. But, God went to great lengths to teach Jonah that God's circle of love is much bigger than Jonah's and ours.

But here is the good news. We can erase the circles we have drawn with our own prejudices and biases and selfishness. We can learn to draw bigger circles. The goal is that one day our circles will be as big as God's.

Now is the time for us to include others in our circles, the circles of those we pray for, our circles of those we check on, our circles of those we really care about. As we do this, we will discover that God has always drawn a circle that included us. God's circle has always included you.

§

- 35 -

In The Beginning And Now (Genesis 1:1-5)

Old Testament scholar Walter Brueggemann wrote, "The first eleven chapters of Genesis are among the most important in Scripture."[9]

The very first words of the Bible are breathtaking if we hear them correctly. They speak to us of God's power and love and of hope.

But, before we look at what this story does mean, it is important to understand what this story is NOT saying. We need to get some incorrect understandings of this story out of our systems. Once our preconceived notions are gone, we are free to hear the truth of the story, maybe for the first time.

First of all, the story of creation is not meant to be a Scientific Manual on the Formation of Planets and Species. The Bible does not speak in scientific technicalities but in doxological descriptions. The Bible speaks of creation like a new parent speaks of the birth of a child: in glowing doxology, not scientific data.

For example, we look at a child and say she has her mother's eyes. Scientifically, that is incorrect. Her mother still has her own eyes. However, science can help us understand genetics and how it happened that her eyes bear a striking resemblance to her mother's. When I say "she has her mother's eyes," you know what I mean. It is still true. I am just stating it poetically, not scientifically.

A friend of mine once told me that it was obvious that my three daughters got their good looks from me. Because their mother still has hers!

The creation stories in the Bible do not seek to answer the question, "HOW did God create the universe?" It seeks to answer the

---

[9] *Walter Brueggemann, Genesis, p.11.*

question, "WHO created the universe?" Not HOW, but WHO. If you come to the story asking the wrong questions, you will get the wrong answers every time.

An added benefit to understanding Genesis theologically, not scientifically, is that it permits scientific theories about creation and the Biblical story of creation to stand side by side without contradiction. No more arguing over science or the Bible. You can believe both.

There are actually two different creation narratives. One is found in Genesis 1:1–2:4. The other is found in Genesis 2:5–25. It deals more with the creation of Adam and Eve and their authority over and responsibility for the rest of creation. Each of these stories has its own theological purpose. We only focus on the first one now.

So, let's look at what the first creation story IS saying to us. *"In the beginning God created the heavens and the earth."*

That is the translation with which we are most familiar. God created. Past tense. Creation is a past event. God created everything in six days, rested on the seventh, and now it is over. It was something God did in the past and completed.

But, there is another way to translate that first verse. It can be translated as a dependent clause: "When God *began to create* the heavens and the earth."[10]

If you translate it that way, then creation is an ongoing event. God didn't start and then stop creating. God started and is still creating. The creation process is ongoing. It is not a done deal. God is not finished. God is still involved in creating the world God intends.

I love the way G. K. Chesterton describes this. He notes that the sun rises every morning. We assume that it does so because God created it that way, set it in motion, and now just sits back and watches creation run. But, what if it is not like that? Have you ever noticed how a child enjoys doing the same thing over and over? When my daughters were little, we would watch the same videos again and

---

[10] *Ibid. p.29.*

again. And as soon as they were over, my daughters would ask for us to play them again. They did the same thing with games.

"Don't you want to do something different?"

"No! Let's do it again!"

Chesterton writes,

> It is possible that God says every morning, 'Do it again' to the sun and every evening, 'Do it again' to the moon? God did not create the daisy and declare it 'one and done.' It may be that God makes every daisy separately but has never got tired of making them. It may be that He has the eternal appetite of infancy, for we have sinned and grown old, and our Father is younger than we. The repetition of Nature may not be a mere coincidence; it may be a theatrical encore.[11]

I love that. God did not create everything and then stop. God is still involved in creation every day. And what if God is inviting us to be involved with God in continuing to create the kind of world God wants? Creation is ongoing, and we are invited to participate.

Picture this scene. There is water everywhere, covering everything, no land in sight. In ancient times water was a symbol of chaos, of fear, of the unknown. The water is covered in darkness, also a symbol of fear, the unknown, even evil.

Across this chaotic water, in the darkness, we find something unexpected. In the midst of the chaos and the darkness, we find the Spirit of God moving over the waters, moving over the chaos. In the midst of the chaos and darkness, God is there!

And into this chaos and darkness, God speaks. God says: *"Let there be light!"*

And light came into being.

---

[11] C. K. Chesterton, *Orthodoxy*, pp.91-92

It is similar to the beginning of the Gospel of John: *"In the beginning was the Word, and the Word was with God, and the Word was God."*

The Word is the light that shines in the darkness. John is repeating the theology and the Good News of the first creation story. Into our darkness and chaos, God speaks, and the light of God shines in the darkness. Genesis is not a story about how the world was made. It is much more important than that. It is a story about the relationship God has to the world that God made.

There was a time when nothing existed. Out of that nothingness, God created everything that exists. But, there was also a time when what did exist was dark and chaotic. And God spoke into that chaos and brought light and structure and form. God can do both.

Imagine living as a Jew in the sixth century BC. You sit in a refugee camp in a foreign land because your land has been invaded and captured by the enemy. Your enemies are celebrating in the streets that their god is stronger than your God. Your once well-ordered life is now in chaos. It is chaos and darkness everywhere.

But, each morning, the sun comes up and shines into your camp. And maybe it reminds you of the story of creation. It reminds you that you serve a God whose Spirit still moves in the midst of chaos and darkness. It reminds you that God still brings light into our darkness.

Creation itself proclaims God's love for us, God's presence with us, and the power that God brings to bear in our lives. This story brings hope, hope that if God can bring order to chaos and light to darkness in the creation of the universe, then God can do it again, into our chaos and our darkness. That is the message of the creation story.

Remember the Baptism of Jesus. Jesus didn't need to be baptized for the reasons we do. He did it as an example for us. He stepped down into the water, just as he stepped down from heaven to earth into the chaos of our world, and he came to bring order and light into our world.

Recently we have experienced a lot of chaos.

There was the chaos and darkness of the COVID pandemic.

There is the chaos and darkness of the racial pandemic.

Many people are experiencing the chaos and darkness of personal pain and loss in their lives as individuals.

Where is God in the midst of all of this?

God is where God always is. The Spirit of God is moving upon the face of the chaos. The Spirit of God is moving upon the face of the darkness. And into our fear, God speaks. "Let there be light."

The story of creation is both Good News and invitation. Good News because the Spirit of God is among us in our chaos and darkness. Good News because God is the One who can bring order and light into our chaos and darkness.

And it is invitation because God is not finished creating. It is an ongoing process, and God has invited us to be involved in it with God. God is still creating a new world. Jesus called it the Kingdom of God. It is a world where God's creation flourishes and where the people God has created can flourish as well. And God invites us to help move in the direction of this new world. We get to be a part of what God is creating.

As in the beginning, God is still creating form out of chaos, light out of darkness, and hope out of whatever we face. God has done it before. My money is on God to do it again.

§

Father Abraham: Mystery (Genesis 22:1-14)

I love the story of Abraham in general. However, it would have been nice if the story had ended with the birth of Isaac. That would have been a nice happy conclusion. But, the thing about reality is that the story continues.

In books and in the movies, when the couple who have been at odds with each other the whole time finally get together and realize their love for one another, the story ends. You walk out of the theater feeling good. But in real life, the couple now have to learn to live together, life continues to happen, and it isn't always happy.

And in books and movies, the hero finally gets rid of all the bad guys, and the world is at peace again. The story ends right there, and we feel good about it. But, in reality (and the sequels), sooner or later, more bad guys arise, and they have to be subdued. The story continues, and there is always a sequel.

So, it is with the story of Isaac. It continues.

This part of the Abraham/Isaac saga is a difficult story. I am reminded of a story about the Protestant reformer Martin Luther. Luther did not like the Book of James in the Bible. He thought its insistence on works presented a problem for his understanding of salvation by faith alone. Martin Luther lobbied to have the Book of James removed from the Bible. But, as it turned out, James was an apostle, and Martin Luther was not, so the Book of James is still there!

When I was in seminary, I had the opportunity to hear Jim Wallis, founder and editor of Sojourner's Magazine. He is also an activist who works on behalf of many justice issues. He held up a Bible that looked rather anemic. Nearly half of the pages seemed to be missing, and it was held together with tape. He had a challenge for us as Christians: if we did not want to take our responsibility to the poor seriously, we should just tear out all of the pages of the Bible that tell us we should. He had done that. He tore out every page of the Bible that talked about helping the poor. The Bible he held up was what was left. And, by the way, about half of it was missing. It was a powerful visual.

I write in my Bible, but I have never intentionally ripped pages out of it. But if I had the opportunity, if God gave me one free veto of any story in the Bible, it would be this one. It is a hard story to hear, and it is even harder to understand.

This story is about a god who tests people and even asks Abraham to sacrifice his only son.

On January 6, 1990, in a small California town, Cristos Valenti took his youngest child, his daughter, to a park. He took her life with a knife. When he was arrested, he told the police that God had told him to do it.[12] No parent can hear this story without getting a lump in your throat. We know that God did not tell him to harm that child. Because we know that the God we serve would never tell anyone to do such a thing.

We know that. So, what do we do with this story of Abraham and Isaac?

Some have explained it this way. The Canaanite culture that surrounded Abraham did practice child sacrifice at this time. So, God told Abraham to do the same thing but then stopped him as a way of showing that God never wanted his people to practice child sacrifice. That is one way to look at it.

This is a dark story. To deal with it, we have come up with a lot of trite answers, and we tend to gloss over the difficulties. The story itself is filled with such tenderness and such pathos. Isaac must have been 12-14 years old. He was the promised son. He was the apple of his father's and mother's eye. He is the one through whom God is

---

[12] Len. Sweet, *Out of the Question . . . Into The Mystery.* p.40.

going to complete his promise. Without Isaac, God's promise is dead. Abraham and Sarah had waited so long for this child. Oh, the joy when he finally arrived. They were so happy, they named him "Laughter." Now, God is going to take him away? To destroy the promise and to harm a child are both contradictory to everything we believe about God.

A few chapters back, when God sent messengers to destroy Sodom and Gomorrah, they stopped by to see Abraham. When Abraham found out what they were going to do, he pleaded with God to spare Sodom and Gomorrah. He begged God to save people he did not even know. But when God asked him to sacrifice his own son, Abraham didn't protest at all.

When it was time to go up the mountain, Abraham carried the fire and the knife. He carried the dangerous things so Isaac could not hurt himself with them. Isaac carried the wood. What a sad picture. Abraham, old and gray, trudging up the mountain with his only child to do the unthinkable.

They move up the hill in silence. Finally, Isaac speaks. "We have everything but the lamb for the sacrifice. Where is the lamb, Papa?"

Abraham swallowed hard and answered, "God, Himself will provide the lamb for the burnt offering, my son."

I wonder why Abraham said that. Was he lying? He didn't want to tell Isaac the truth, so he came up with the first story he could think of? Like, when we tell people everything is going to be alright, even when we don't really think it is.

Or maybe it was wishful thinking. Abraham was hoping that God would provide because if God didn't provide, then everything Abraham had lived his life for was gone.

Or, maybe it was a statement of faith? Just maybe, somehow, in spite of everything, Abraham still believed that God was faithful. He really believed that God would provide for them.

This is the key to the whole story. Is God faithful? Will God provide? Can we count on God when the stakes are high?

They reached the top. We are not told if Isaac struggled or willingly submitted to Abraham's wishes. But, Abraham tied up his son, laid him on the wood, and attempted the unimaginable. He raised the knife high above his head. Then, Abraham heard the voice of an angel. It certainly sounded like an angel to Isaac!

He said, "Abraham! Abraham!"

Abraham stopped and said, "I am here." The angel told him not to lay a hand on the boy. The knife fell to the ground. Isaac started to breathe again.

Abraham looked up, and he saw a ram caught by his horns in some thick brush. We are not told whether it was there all along and Abraham just noticed it or whether it got caught at that moment. Either way, God provided it. Isaac was released and replaced with the ram. Blood flowed on the wood. But it wasn't human blood. Isaac was spared. Abraham was spared. In a real sense, God was spared.

It is interesting that the Scripture says that after the sacrifice was offered, Abraham went down the mountain, met up with his servants, and went home. Isaac is not mentioned. Maybe as soon as Abraham untied him, Isaac ran off and didn't stay around for the sacrifice. Who could blame him if he did? Maybe he decided to just go home on his own. The Bible never records another conversation between Abraham and Isaac. I don't imagine they spoke much after that. Some Jewish people see Isaac as the Father of all holocaust survivors. He was the first innocent young Jew to escape from being sacrificed.

It is a troubling story, this God who tests his followers as if our lives are not hard enough already. Like Job, Abraham is given a promise and great blessings only to be faced with losing it all. We don't like this testing. It does not fit neatly into our image of God.

Some would like to turn this story into just some sort of typology about Jesus and the cross, proclaiming how God would not let Abraham kill Isaac, but God would not spare his own son. Somehow a god who kills his own son doesn't give me any comfort either. I am aware that most people only understand what happened on the cross in terms of sacrifice and killing. If the idea of God killing his own son has never sat right with you, you are not alone. There are other ways of understanding the cross and other atonement theories that can give us a fresh look at what happened on Calvary. The theory of substitutional atonement is the one most Evangelicals grew up with. Most of us were only taught that one, and many think it is the only way to understand Jesus' death on the cross. There are many good books that explain these different theories, and even a good google search can help you get an idea of other ways of understanding atonement.

We are caught somewhere in the middle of the mystery of this God who tests us but who also provides for us. God will not be controlled. We can't put God into our little boxes and figure everything out. God is God. God owes us no explanation. And God gives none. There is a mystery to this God we serve.

The traditional understanding of this story is that it was to test Abraham's faith. To see if Abraham really loved God enough, really trusted God enough, to be obedient to whatever God asked him to do. In the end, Abraham passed the test and proved to be faithful. It makes a great Bible story.

But, none of us can identify with that. The truth is, if God told me to sacrifice one of my children or do harm to any of my children, I would say, "NO!" "NO!" And so would you. As a matter of fact, I am not so sure I would want to keep serving a god who would ever ask such a thing. So, that traditional understanding doesn't work for me.

Here is what I take away from the mystery of this story. Abraham was not the only one tested that day. God made a promise to Abraham. If Isaac died, that promise would die too. For me, it is not about Abraham passing the test. It is about God passing the test. God proved that in the most hopeless situations he would provide.

God proved he could be trusted.[13] We need to know that in the midst of difficulties and difficult situations, when the stakes couldn't be higher, God can be trusted. God will provide.

Years ago, I read a story about an African-American pastor. He had a little seven-year-old daughter. It was the decade of the sixties, and the school in their town was being integrated for the first time. He knew her first day of school would be a frightening day. So, he held her hand and walked with her into the building. Mobs of angry, white people lined the sidewalk and shouted all manner of insults and curses at them. The little girl was scared, but she bravely held his hand as he walked her into the school.

Years later, he told that story of that day. He said, "I felt like Abraham." He needed God to provide. He said the day before he prayed and prayed. Someone asked him what did he pray. He said, "I prayed, dear Lord, God, let the horns be long and the brush be thick. Please provide for my little girl." And God did.

We serve a God that we cannot explain. We serve a God whose ways are different than our ways. But we serve a God who is faithful. We serve a God who provides when the situation is hopeless and the stakes are high. God passes the test. God is faithful, and in the end, that, more than anything else, is what I need to know most. Not that Abraham is faithful, but that God is faithful. I need to know that God provides. This story says that God is, and God does. Amen.

§

---

[13] *Walter Brueggemann, Genesis, p.194.*

Tell No One (Mark 9:2-9)

At the beginning of Mark's Gospel, we observe Jesus being baptized. At first, Jesus is just standing there, knee-deep in the muddy Jordan like everyone else who came to be dunked by John. He was just another person in the crowd. But, when he was baptized, something extraordinary happened. Jesus went down in the water like everyone else. But, when he came up out of the water, things were different. The water rolled off of his face like everyone else, but then something amazing happened. The heavens opened, and the Spirit descended on him like a dove. Then a voice spoke from heaven and said, *"You are my Son whom I love; with you I am well pleased."*

That didn't happen to anyone else getting baptized. This set Jesus apart from all of the other people drip drying in the sun that day. The voice singled him out. Fred Craddock paraphrased what the voice said like this: *"This is who he really is."*[14]

He looked like just another man in mid-life crisis getting baptized. But he was more than that. He was God's son. *"This is who he really is."*

The next time we hear a voice from heaven identifying who Jesus really is is when he and three disciples go up on a mountain, and Jesus is transformed (transfigured) in front of them.

Right before they went up on the mountain, Jesus predicted his death. He told them quite plainly that he was going to die. Peter didn't want to believe him. All that talk about death scared them. Jesus took them up on the mountain, and there he was transformed, transfigured right in front of them.

---

[14] *Fred Craddock, Collected Sermons, p.123.*

Then, they heard that voice a second time *"This is my Son, whom I love. Listen to him!"*

You are going to see him suffer and die, just like he told you. But, look at him now! *"This is who he really is!"*

It is an experience that gave the disciples strength for the weeks to come.

They saw him arrested.

They saw him beaten.

They saw him crucified.

They saw the place where they laid his dead body. *"But this is who he really is."*

The one you see transfigured on the mountain. *"This is who he really is!"*

It gave them strength.

This story is always told the last Sunday in Epiphany in the lectionary before we enter the season of Lent. We remember his sacrifice. We remember his suffering. We remember his death.

But, *"this is who he really is!"*

We hear this voice speak to us at Jesus' baptism, at the very beginning of his public ministry. We hear this voice again at Jesus' transfiguration, at the beginning of his passion. It is the beginning of the events we remember during Lent.

There are a lot of similarities between the Transfiguration of Jesus and the experience of Moses when he went up on a mountain.[15] In both instances, the Scripture mentioned six days. They waited six days between the last event and the day they went up on the mountain. (Ex. 24:16) A cloud covers the mountain. (Ex. 24:16). God speaks from the cloud. (Ex. 24:16) Moses had three companions with him when he started up the mountain: Aaron, Nadab, and Abihu. But his three companions chickened out. Moses' appearance was transformed while he was on the mountain. (Ex. 34:30). His face became

---

[15] *Alan Culpepper, Mark, p.293*

radiant. The reaction of those who saw Moses transformed and the three disciples who saw Jesus transfigured was the same. They were scared. (Ex. 34:30)

You might think that Peter, James, and John would be better prepared for what they saw. They knew the stories of Moses going up on the mountain. They had heard about what happened to him. They had seen Jesus perform miracles. They had seen him heal the sick. They had seen him drive out demons. They had seen him heal a man with leprosy. They had seen him heal a man who was paralyzed. They had even seen him raise a little girl from the dead. You would think something like this would not be so shocking. But it was.

They were not ready for it. They were terrified. Scared to death. Like Moses' buddies, if they had known what was going to happen, I am not so sure they would have gone.

"Jesus, thanks a lot for inviting us to go up the mountain with you, but I need to tie some flies. Big fishing trip coming up. Things to do. But we will be with you in spirit!"

Jesus was transformed right before their very eyes. And as we hear this story, he is transformed right before our very eyes too. We are there with them on the mountain. We see what they see. Jesus' clothes became dazzling white. It was as if Jesus was glowing. Then, out of nowhere, standing by him were Elijah and Moses. They were having a conversation. As if any of this is normal.

Many people say that Moses represents the law and Elijah represents the prophets. But, whatever they represent, there they are, in a strange, surreal, other-worldly kind of scene. It looked like something right out of Stranger Things.

Some people, when they are frightened, are too scared to move and too scared to speak. They cannot say a word. Peter was not so lucky. Apparently, when Peter was frightened, he started talking. He shouldn't have. But he did. He didn't know what was going on. He didn't know what to say. It was the fear speaking.

"Rabbi, I am so glad we are here!" Peter said, with his knees knocking. "Let's build three booths, one for you, one for Moses, and one for Elijah." Peter wasn't sure why he said that. It seemed like a good idea at the time.

I have a friend who tells the story of when he was in Middle School and was scared to death of girls. There was a girl he had a crush on. He had a chance to talk to her one day, and he was scared to death. He didn't know what to say. He blurted out, "Do you like bread?"

Later, he was kicking himself over saying something so stupid. He had waited for the chance to talk to her, and he blew it. His fear made him say something dumb. That is how I see what Peter said. Some people want to know the meaning behind what Peter was thinking. I don't think there is one. It was fear talking. Peter just blurted out something because he was scared and he didn't know what to do.

That is when the cloud showed up. God, in grace, rescued Peter from himself. God interrupted him and said, "This is my Son, whom I love. Listen to him!" "Peter. Stop. Shhhh. Just listen to him. See with your eyes what is happening. Listen with your heart to what is happening."

"This is who he really is."

Suddenly, everything was back to normal. The cloud disappeared. Jesus' appearance was back to normal. Moses and Elijah were gone. They walked back down the mountain together in silence. Peter wanted to say something, but he refrained. Then Jesus spoke up and said, "Tell no one what you have seen until after the resurrection."

"Tell no one." It sounds like rather odd advice. After an experience like that, I'll bet Peter, James and John couldn't wait to tell somebody what they had seen. People like to point out that this fits a pattern in Mark. Jesus often healed people in Mark's Gospel and then told them to tell no one. The Messianic Secret and all that.

I think there is more to it than that. "Tell no one until after the resurrection." "After the resurrection, you can tell this story. But, not until then. Don't tell this story until after the resurrection."

They didn't understand who Jesus was, not really. They didn't understand what he had come to do. If they had run out and told the story of the Transfiguration, they would have gotten it all wrong. They still didn't really understand that there was a cross to come. There was suffering to come. There were times of despair and hopelessness to come.

If they had told the story then, they would have told it as just another dazzling miracle story. Just another victory along the way. Just Jesus being awesome again. There would be carnival music in the background, and it would just be another story about Jesus, the conquering Messiah. They would have told it all wrong.

So, they had to wait. They had to experience a few other things. They had to know the fear of hearing the footsteps of the guards coming into the garden to arrest Jesus. They had to experience the hopelessness of seeing his dead body taken off the cross and put into a grave. They had to know the fear and the incredible joy of seeing Jesus stand before them. Alive! Resurrected from the dead. Then, they could tell the story. Then they would understand what had happened up on the mountain. Then, they could tell the story properly.

I have recently told some stories about some of the pain I have experienced in my life. They were stories that were hard to share publicly. Sometimes it takes years to be able to tell a story. Sometimes it takes a long time to understand what happened to us. Some stories take a long time to tell.

This is why you should never discount a woman's story of sexual abuse that happened years ago. Or a man's either, for that matter. I hear people say, "Well, why didn't she say something then?" It's because some stories take a long time to tell. You can't tell them right away. You have to experience some things before you can understand and speak about other things you have experienced.

Wait until after the resurrection. Then you can tell the story. Then you can tell it right.

Honestly, I still don't think we know what to do with this Transfiguration story. What does it mean? How does it apply to us? That is why I am going to ask you to not rush to any conclusions. Don't go telling the story too soon. Hold it in your thoughts. Mull it over in your mind for a while. Take it with you through the Season of Lent. Think about it as you kneel and receive ashes on your forehead and hear the words, "Remember that you are dust and to dust you shall return." Think about it as we experience again the fear, the love, the courage and the sacrifice of the Last Supper and the prayer in the garden. Think about it as we experience standing at the foot of the cross where Jesus dies for us. Think about it as we stand in the locked room with the disciples and see for ourselves the risen Christ. Let all of those experiences wash over us.

Then. Maybe, then, we will understand it a little better. Maybe then, we will find our tongue. Maybe then, after all of these years, we will be able to tell the story of who Jesus really is. Maybe then we will be able to tell the story right.

§

Living In the Shadows

We would prefer to do most of our living in the sunshine. We like it when things are bright and cheery. Unfortunately, life has some shadow moments as well. There are times when things don't go our way. There are times when we face complications that range from frustrating to tragic. Those are the times we live in the shadows.

The Biblical story does not hide the difficulties that people—even Godly people—face in their lives. The stories of the women and men of the Scripture are stories of how they made it through the bad times as well as the good.

In the Christian year, along with all of the seasons of celebration, comes the season of Lent. Appropriately it falls during the winter. Winter, with its short days, long and cold nights, and trees with leafless branches, is often a symbol for life when it is most dreary and barren. Lent is a time of repentance, a time of facing the evil and hurt in our world and in our own lives. It is a reminder that as Jesus had to face the cross, the rest of us will experience times of difficulty and confusion in our lives as well.

The best thing about hearing others' stories of struggle and broken family relationships is that it reminds us that we are not alone. These stories help us realize that if they can get through those tough times, so can we. These are stories of people dealing with broken relationships and broken lives who find the hope and strength to keep going until the sun comes out again. May they inspire you to do the same.

§

Got The Blues (Psalm 13:1-6)

I've been run down and lied to,
And I don't know why I let that mean
woman make me a fool.
She took all my money, wrecked my new car.
Now she is with one of my good time buddies,
They're drinking in some cross-town bar.
Sometimes I feel, sometimes I feel,
I feel like I've been tied to the whippin' post.[16]

Now that is the blues, courtesy of the Allman Brothers. "Sometimes I feel like I've been tied to the whippin' post." Have you ever felt that way? Sure, you have. We all have. Some of you may feel that way now.

The blues are a popular genre of music because we can identify with it. There are times when we all need to sing the blues. Certainly not all the time, but sometimes. Sometimes it helps, especially those times when you feel like you have been tied to the whippin' post.

The Blues are not a new genre of music. We have a particular brand of Blues that is uniquely American. However, the Blues go back a long way in history. They at least go back to the pages of the Hebrew Scriptures.

The Book of Psalms is the Songbook of the Bible. It is filled with different kinds of psalms: praise psalms, royal psalms, road-trip psalms, wisdom psalms. But, the largest category of psalms is called

---

[16] *Gregg L. Allman, "Whipping Post," LyricFind.*

the lament psalms, or as I like to call them, The Blues Psalms. The Blues Psalms make up one-fourth of the psalter.

Since 25% of the psalms are Blues Psalms, I find it curious that our hymnals and worship choruses don't reflect that kind of variety. When it comes to worship, the music available to us is pretty heavy on praise songs and pretty light on the blues.

Old Testament theologian Walter Brueggemann calls the lament psalms, or Blues Psalms, psalms of disorientation.[17] These are the songs we pray when we feel disoriented, when life is just not going the way we believe it should. When we find ourselves disoriented, we don't want to sing happy songs. They just don't ring true.

And, in the words of an English Theologian, Elton John;

> *Guess there are times when we need to share a little pain,*
> *And suffer just enough to sing the blues,*
> *Sad songs, they say so much.[18]*

Often, we try so hard to make church a happy place that we fail to make it an authentic place. These Blues Psalms remind us that God is there when things are going great, and God is there when things are not going so well. We can trust God when things are good, and we can trust God when they're not. God loves us, and God is with us, whether our tears are tears of joy or pain.

The Blues Psalms are the psalms of people who are hurting. They question and often accuse God. They are raw and honest. They have a lot to teach us about God and ourselves.

To get the full impact, turn to Psalm 13. It follows the pattern or template of Blues Psalms perfectly. The pattern is this: The Address, The Complaint, The Petition, The Confession of Trust, and The Vow of Praise. Let's look at how the Psalmist puts it together.

First is the *Address:* "How long, LORD?" In the Bible, the word "LORD" is in all capital letters. That is to let you know that in the Hebrew text from which it was translated, the word used here was

---

[17] *Walter Brueggemann,* The Message Of The Psalms, *p.51.*
[18] *Bernie Taupin/Elton John, "Sad Songs Say So Much," LyricFind.*

the word "Yahweh." God's name. When it is a capital "L," and the rest of the letters are lower case, it is the translation of the word "Adonai," which means "Lord." Even though the psalmist feels abandoned by God, he doesn't talk *about* God; he talks *to* God. He knows God is still with him, and he speaks directly to God.

When Jesus was on the cross, he cried out, "My God, my God, why have you forsaken me!" Jesus is speaking directly to God, knowing God is there with him. It is just the same with the psalmist. He also speaks to God, knowing that God has not left, even if he doesn't feel God's presence.

Next comes the *Complaint.* The psalmist blames God for his problems because it seems as if God has forgotten him. It feels like Yahweh has turned his face away from him. He has sorrow in his heart, and his enemies have triumphed over him.

"How long, Yahweh? How long?"

We have all prayed that prayer, haven't we? "How long, Lord, will I have to wait until I can find a job that is meaningful?" "How long, Lord, before I can provide for my family the way I want to?" "How long, Lord, do I have to wait to find a meaningful relationship with someone who will love me?" "How long, Lord, before I can get through this painful experience and move on to the next chapter in my life?" "How long, Lord, will I be sick and tired?" "How long, Lord, before we stop asking, "How long?" The Psalmist says it four times. "How long, Lord?"

The *Petition.* The psalmist's petition is about three things; God, self, and others.

It is about God because God seems absent and doesn't seem to be concerned about what the psalmist is going through.

It is about himself because he is hurting.

It is about others. In this case, his enemies or—translated literally—his distressors, the ones causing at least some of his pain.

Our petitions always revolve around these three things.

Even though he accuses God of not caring and of being absent, he keeps right on talking to God. He keeps right on praying. Whatever he is going through does not cause him to lose faith. He keeps praying to the God who doesn't seem to be listening.

Then something happens. What happened was he waited. He waited in the darkness. He waited in the disorientation. We don't know how long he waited. It may have been a short wait. It may have been a long wait. After you have laid out your complaints to God, there is no court of appeal. Sometimes there is nothing you can do but wait. Wait until God responds.[19]

The wait is hard. Some of you may be waiting right now. You have poured out your complaint or your prayers to God, and now you are waiting for God to respond. You are waiting for God to answer your prayer. You are waiting for God to make his presence known to you. You are waiting for God to lift the sorrow in your heart.

I wish I could tell you that the wait will not be long, but I don't know that. But, I do know this; you don't have to wait alone. On our good days, this is a part of what it means to be the church. If you invite others into your suffering, they will wait with you. We will not speak to each other in clichés. We will not offer each other simplistic answers. We may not have any answers at all. We will not make each other sing happy songs. We will wait together until God acts.

Finally, the psalm gives way to the *Confession of Trust* and the *Vow of Praise*. Something changed. We don't know if God answered his prayer or if the psalmist is still waiting. His focus is now on God's unfailing love and God's goodness. We don't know if God changed his circumstances or if God changed the psalmist. Either way, it is a miracle. Either way, it results in praise to the God who is faithful.

In the lectionary, this psalm is read on the Sunday we read the story of Abraham's attempted sacrifice of his son, Isaac, found in Genesis 22. Isaac was the son God had promised Abraham and Sarah. A promise both of them had waited on for a long, long time. Then

---

[19] *Walter Brueggemann, The Message of the Psalms. P.59.*

Abraham believed God wanted him to sacrifice Isaac. Abraham did not understand. He was filled with sorrow. After tying the boy to the altar and preparing to do the unthinkable, God intervened. An angel put a stop to things, and Abraham saw a ram caught in the bushes, the acceptable substitute for Isaac.

As I have said earlier, I think the story is less about demonstrating Abraham's faithfulness and more about demonstrating God's faithfulness. The psalmist and the story of Abraham and Isaac tell us the same thing. In the midst of our sorrow, God is faithful. Gods' love for us is unfailing. God is good.

Even when we are waiting, we can trust God because God loves us. You know God is good—even when you feel like you've been tied to a whippin' post.

A good friend of mine reminded me that there is a major difference between the Blues Songs of the Allman Brothers, B.B. King, and other American Blues songs and the Blues Psalms from the Scripture.[20] Blues songs often end with us tied to the whippin' post. It is a catharsis that helps us deal with our pain.

The Blues Psalms do not leave us there. They remind us of a God who loves us and unties us. They offer us hope. They move us from a pity party to a celebration of life.

§

---

[20] *Conversation with Chuck Holmes, October 15, 2021.*

The Story of Two Sons And Their Father[21]: Part I (Luke 15)

The Return Of The Prodigal Son

This is one of my favorite stories in the Bible. To do it justice, we will examine each of the three main characters individually

But before we start, we need to get a new mindset. For most of us, the story is very familiar, and when we hear it again, we really don't listen. Let's hear it again for the first time.

There is a famous portrait titled *"The Return Of The Prodigal Son."* It was painted by Rembrandt, which is an interesting story in itself. This is one of the last works he painted in his old age before he died. Rembrandt was quite the rager in his day, a free-spirited young man. His life theme song was "Born to be Wild." Later in his life, he endured several personal tragedies and lost his wealth. Many see this painting as a personal reflection of his own return to God, his own coming home. If that is true, then there is no wonder why he chose to paint the prodigal son; There is no story that better depicts our returning to God.

There are three main characters in this story: two sons and their father. First, we will consider the youngest son, the one we often call the prodigal son.

> *There was a man who had two sons. The younger son said to his father, "Father, give me my share of the estate." So he divided his property between them. Not*

---

[21] *Many ideas in this series of stories from what we know as the Parable of the Prodigal Son were inspired by Henri Nouwen's book, The Return of The Prodigal Son.*

*long after that, the younger son got together all he had, set
off for a distant country, and there squandered his wealth
in wild living.*

The title of Rembrandt's painting is *"The Return of the Prodigal Son,"*
but before there can be a return, there must be a leaving. When a
child leaves home, there is always some pain for the parent, even in
the best of circumstances. But here, the circumstances are not very
good. We can imagine the pain the father must have felt. Some of
you don't have to imagine; you have felt it.

First, the younger son asked for his portion of his inheritance, the
money and property that would be passed on to him when his father
died. It was the equivalent of one of your children saying to you,
"Dad, give me whatever you were going to put in your will for me
now. I can't sit around forever and wait for you to die! I need it
now."

Surprisingly, the father granted his son's request. He also gave his
older son his share, even though he didn't ask for it. Notice, right
from the beginning of the story, the father shows the same love for
the older son as he does the younger. I can't imagine saying that to
my Dad, and I can't imagine him saying yes. Actually, I can't imagine
that they would have been allowed to print my Dad's response in the
Bible.

When the check cleared the bank, the younger son took off. He
had everything he came for from his family, but he saw no responsibility to use any of it in a way to help the family which had nurtured
and cared for him from his birth. His was strictly an entitlement men-
tality. "It's all about me!" So, he took everything he could.

Then, he left for a far country. It wasn't enough to just get away
from his father's house. He wanted to get as far away as he could. A
far or distant country implies that he rejected most of the things his
father held dear. We discover later that this country is a Gentile country. By going there and adopting its culture, he rejects his father's values and his father's faith.

As you read the story, you have to stop and ask why? Why leave a home where you are loved? Why leave and go to a distant place? Why leave home? And the only answer I know is that he left home for the same reason we all leave home. And now I am not talking about our physical homes, but our home in God's family, our home in God's presence.

God created each of us because God loves us and wants to live life in relationship with us. But, all of us leave. We leave by choice. We decide that what the world has to offer us looks more exciting. We take everything God has given us, our inheritance, our intellect, our talents, our abilities, and off we go. Far away from God, using them for ourselves, not the One who gave them to us. And in that leaving, there is pain. Like any parent, God weeps for us when we leave home. But, God loves us. God lets us go.

And so, the younger son left. He left his Father's presence much as I left and as you left, believing that wealth, pleasure, success—fill in the blank—would make him happier than being with his father.

And for a while, he had a blast. While the money held up, at least, he was having a good time. He experienced everything youth, wealth and pleasure had to offer. But, he found out something unexpected. The fun was short-term. When the money ran out, the fun ran out, and the friends ran out. It was all gone, and he was still empty. He had thought that getting away from his father and living it up would be the greatest thing ever. He didn't have to live under his father's rules anymore. But, he soon discovered the heartache his father's rules had kept him from experiencing. He now knew an emptiness he had never known before.

And we understand. We leave God and the life God has for us to do life on our own. And often, it is good, at least for a while. But, sooner or later, we discover the heartache God tried to help us avoid. We find an emptiness that can't be filled by the stuff we have or do. We look for peace and purpose and can't seem to find it. It's like the old country song says, "We look for love in all the wrong places." We want to be loved. But the love we find in our culture is filled with "ifs." I promise to love you "if" you are attractive enough, "if" you are wealthy enough, "if" you are athletic enough, "if" you are intelligent enough, "if" you produce enough. Our culture's love is always conditional. And we want to be loved so badly that we are willing to play all the games. We will wear the right clothes, get the right look, try so hard to do all the "right" things. We try so hard to fit in and be accepted. We are looking for unconditional love. But we never find it in the culture. Often it is not until we have squandered much that we realize we cannot find what we are looking for in the places we are looking.

> *After he had spent everything, there was a severe famine in that whole country; and he began to be in need. So he went and hired himself out to a citizen of that country, who sent him to his fields to feed pigs. He longed to fill his stomach with the pods that the pigs were eating, but no one gave him anything. When he came to his senses, he said, "How many of my father's hired men have food to spare, and here I am starving to death! I will set out and go back to my father and say to him: 'Father, I have sinned against heaven and against you. I am no longer worthy to be called your son; make me like one of your hired men.'" So he got up and went to his father.*

The day finally came when the young son realized he was in a terrible predicament. His money was gone, and when he thought things couldn't get any worse, the country where he had chosen to live experienced a dire famine. He got a job on a pig farm, feeding pigs. I grew up on a farm. We had pigs. We raised them, and we slaughtered some in the fall. Several years ago, my daughters were in 4-H. My two oldest daughters each raised a pig for the county fair. It brought back a lot of memories from my childhood. I like pigs, as far as animals go, but the aroma from a pigpen is a distinct experience. There is truly nothing like it. The smell cannot be washed out of your boots or shoes. Once you wear a pair into the pigpen, they can never be used for anything else.

Apart from the smell, Jewish people did not eat or even touch pigs. For a Jewish boy to be feeding pigs for a living was a social disgrace. He was so hungry that as he fed the pigs he wished he could eat some of the food the pigs were eating. Some translations say he fed them "Pods." It was actually a kind of fruit that grows on a carob tree. These days it is commonly called "St. John's Bread." They didn't taste very good, and so only the poorest people ate them. Everyone else used them to feed their animals. It was like longing for some Alpo.

Then one day, he assessed his situation. He was starving. He was trudging his way through the pigpen doing his dirty work when, the Bible says, *"he came to his senses."* The proper translation of the Greek word here is "Duh!" He realized that back at his father's house, even the servants had it better than he did. At this point, he realized three things.

1. He had blown it and was genuinely sorry.
2. He didn't deserve to be a part of his father's family
3. He will return to his father anyway.

Standing ankle-deep in pig . . . pen, he realized, "I've blown it. I have taken everything my father has given me, and I have blown it." Those last verses where he plans to tell his father, "I have sinned against you, and I am not worthy to be your son . . ." shows the depth of his sorrow over what he has done. He is not just sorry that times got hard. He realized that he had made a mistake and would make different decisions if he had the opportunity to do it again. This is what the Bible calls "repentance." Not just being sorry that you got caught or that things didn't work out, but sorry for what you have done. There is a difference between repentance and damage control.

Several years ago, I read that the IRS set up a special fund called the "cheater's account." The idea was to provide a service to people who have cheated on their taxes and feel guilty about it. People who have cheated on their taxes could send in money anonymously to this account. The purpose was to help people who were struggling with a guilty conscience. And to receive at least some of the taxes owed. The story goes that the IRS received a letter that read, "I have cheated on my taxes for years, and I feel so guilty I can't sleep at night. Enclosed, please find a money order for $10,000. P.S. If I still can't sleep, I'll send in the rest of what I owe."[22]

That is sort of a self-serving deal. But this younger son felt real repentance. He was sorry, and he wanted his father to know. He realized he was wrong. He left with an attitude of entitlement, but he returned realizing no one owes him anything. He returned looking for nothing except his father. With precious few words, Luke tells us about something that changed this young man's life forever: *"So, he got up and went to his father."*

The younger son realized that in spite of all he had done, he still had a father, a father to whom he could return. That is the key difference between this son who returned and many others who never come home. He still understood his identity as a child of his father, no matter how tarnished it was.

It's like this: Judas betrayed Jesus. But, so did Peter. Peter betrayed Jesus when he denied that he knew him. Both left home. But, for some reason, Judas could no longer hold on to the truth that he was God's child. He didn't believe that he could come home, and so—in despair—he hung himself. He never tried to go back home. Peter, in the midst of his despair, remembered that he was a child of God, and he returned to God with many tears. Judas chose death, and Peter chose life. Peter knew he had a heavenly parent to whom he could return. So many sons and daughters forget that. They think they are too far away. But we are never too far away to come back home. We always have a heavenly parent waiting to receive us. You can always come home.

---

[22] *John Ortberg, Love Beyond Reason, p.199.*

It's a message we can never forget: we can always come home.

Maybe you feel far away from God. It could be that you feel the distance between you and God is too great to make up at this point in your life. Hear the Good News. God wants to welcome you back as God's child. You are never too far away to come home. No matter what you have done or how long you have been gone, you have a loving, heavenly parent to whom you can come home. But, you have to choose. God has already chosen to accept you. But you have to choose to begin the journey. At some point, you have to decide to "get up and go to God, your heavenly parent."

Now, the younger son didn't make it home in a day. It was a long journey from the far country. He had lots of time to think, to do some soul-searching. It could be that you need to do that as well. But, start the journey now. Don't keep putting it off. Take the first step by praying and asking God to forgive you for whatever it is you believe separates you from God. Then talk with someone you trust as a Christian. It is a journey. It is a process. It doesn't happen in a day.

In Rembrandt's famous portrait, the young man returns a poor man. He left home with money, health, honor, reputation. He returned having squandered it. His head is shaved. In those days, a shaved head was a symbol of slavery or servanthood. His father and brother are dressed in rich red robes while he is dressed in a dirty, torn, yellow garment. His left foot is bare, and the sandal on his right foot is broken.

He wasn't the son he was when he left. But, the father welcomed him home. He threw a party for him and celebrated his return. The greatest lesson I think we can learn from the younger son is this: *he knew he could come home, and he did.*

All of us can identify with at least part of this story. Those of us who are followers of Christ know too well that we have left home. We have all been prodigal sons and daughters. We celebrate with this younger son. We understand and celebrate the joy he found when one day he decided to come home. He didn't know what to expect. But, like all of the rest of us, he got more than he expected.

Some of you may only identify with the first part of the story though. You only know about the leaving. You only know about living in the far country. Why not experience the rest of the story? Why not find out what it is like to be welcomed home. You have a heavenly parent who is waiting to welcome you back into the family. God has done everything up to this point. Now the ball is in your court. You have to decide to come home. Don't ever forget. You can always come home.

§

The Story Of Two Sons And Their Father: Part II: (Luke 15)

The Other Lost Son

Most people refer to this whole parable as the parable of the prodigal son. But, if you really listen to the story, you discover that it is not a story about one son but two sons. The story begins, "A man had two sons." Not one son, but two sons are lost. They are just lost in different ways. And quite frankly, I think the older son's journey back home can be the most difficult. Difficult, because he doesn't realize he has left.

Back to Rembrandt's portrait. On the right-hand side of the portrait stands the older son. Externally, he resembles his father: red robe, beard. But, his hands are not extended to welcome his brother, like his father's hands. His hands are clasped, head down. He doesn't seem to enjoy the fact that his younger brother has come home. He isn't at all happy about it. Rembrandt's painting differs from the biblical account. In the story that Jesus told, the older son doesn't even come inside the house. He refused to come in. So, let's hear the second part of the story as Jesus told it. The younger brother took his part of the estate and squandered it and has now returned. The father welcomed him and threw him a party. The older brother was out in the field and had no idea what was going on.

> *Meanwhile, the older son was in the field. When he came near the house, he heard music and dancing. So he called one of the servants and asked him what was going on. "Your brother has come," he replied, "and your father*

*has killed the fattened calf because he has him back safe
and sound." The older brother became so angry and
refused to go in. So his father went out and pleaded with
him, but he answered his father, "Look! All these years
I've been slaving for you and never disobeyed your orders.
Yet you never gave me even a young goat so I could celebrate with my friends. But when this son of yours who
has squandered your property with prostitutes comes
home, you kill the fattened calf for him!"*

The younger son left home looking for happiness and excitement,
and he got lost. The older son stayed at home, was obedient, but
somehow got lost too. We don't like to admit it, but those of us who
have been Christians for a while, if we are not careful, identify more
with the older son than with the younger. Someone said, "The trick
after coming home as the younger son is to not turn into the older
brother." The older son is just as far from his father and his father's
heart as the younger son was. He suffers from a different kind of
lostness. It is a lostness that is harder to understand.

When his brother came home, he was in the field working. Where
else would he be? He is the obedient, dutiful son, working hard for
his father. But, when he gets word that his brother has come home
and his father has thrown a party, the signs of his lostness surface.
The signs of his younger brother's lostness were so easy to spot. He
misused his money, his time, his friends, his own body. He rebelled
against morality. He gave in to greed and lust. He went out and
trashed all of his father's values. It is easy to see his lostness.

But, the older son is obedient, dutiful, law-abiding, moral, hard-
working. Outwardly, he is a perfect son. But, inwardly, he is very different from his father. Inwardly he is just as lost as his brother was.
Here are the signs of his lostness.

1. RESENTMENT

When confronted with his father's joy, all that pours out of the older son is resentment. He can't celebrate with his brother because he is too busy feeling sorry for himself. He resents his younger brother. Maybe he resents that his younger brother experienced things he never did. While he avoided sin, his younger brother swam in it. And even though he knows he made the better choice, he resents having always been the dependable one.

He is like many Christians today who obey God out of fear, not love. They look at wayward brothers and sisters and condemn them for the way they live. Yet, inside, they are envious and resentful that they are too afraid of God to try some of those things themselves. They obey out of fear and not love, and it causes resentment.

Look at his complaint to his father. "Look! All these years I've been slaving for you and never disobeyed your orders." He sees his obedience as slavery. He doesn't enjoy being with his father or doing his father's work. It is a duty. It is an obligation. He resents all the work he feels he has to do.

Again, how many followers of Christ today serve in the church and obey God, but it is nothing to them but a burden. There is no joy in it. They do it because they are supposed to, not because they want to. Service to God and obedience to God is just sort of slavery. An obligation they had just as soon get out of if only their guilt would let them.

The Bible also says he became angry. Resentment and anger are close friends. Where you find one, you will often find the other. He was angry and resentful because his brother ran off and did all of the things you are not supposed to do, then came home and was welcomed and celebrated. He felt like he had never left, had dutifully done the hard work, and was never welcomed or celebrated. He was angry because he never left and never enjoyed being home.

Henri Nouwen writes,

> There is so much resentment among the 'just'
> and the 'righteous.' There is so much judgment,
> condemnation, and prejudice among the 'saints.'
> There is so much anger among the people who
> are so concerned about avoiding 'sin.[23]

Wow. Just look at our own culture and see how true that is. Why is it that way? If we are not careful, it seems, the harder we try to obey God, the more we resent those who don't. And we even resent the love and grace with which God embraces them when they come home. The older son never left the property, but he was as far away from the father as the younger son had ever been.

2. LACK OF JOY

Besides his resentment, his lostness shows in his lack of joy over his brother's return. They started the party without him, and he felt excluded. He is focused on himself and feels he has never gotten his due. His father is filled with joy over his brother's return, but he can't seem to muster any joy himself. It is hard to rejoice over what God has done for others when you are upset over what God hasn't done for you.

Who is the older brother in the story? Let's go back to the very first verses in Luke 15.

> Now the tax collectors and "sinners" were all gathering
> around to hear him. But the Pharisees and the teachers
> of the law muttered, "This man welcomes sinners and
> eats with them."

The tax collectors and "sinners" heard this story with joy because they understood that they were the wayward sons and daughters who would be welcomed back by God if only they would return to him. But the Pharisees and teachers of the law, who couldn't understand

---

[23] *Nouwen, p.71.*

why Jesus welcomed and ate with sinners, found themselves in the role of the older brother who can't understand why his father would welcome home and throw a party for his wayward brother. They understood that they were the older brother in the story.

It doesn't stop there though. Throughout history, religious folks have found themselves in the role of the older brother every time their service to God becomes a duty instead of a privilege. Every time we serve out of fear and duty instead of love. Every time our obedience and purity come at the price of our growing resentment and joylessness.

Let's go ahead and take it the last painful step. We veteran churchgoers often have more older brother in us than we care to admit. Instead of genuinely loving God's wayward sons and daughters, we often resent them. We resent our brothers and sisters for leaving us to do all the work. We resent serving in all the ministries and giving all the money while others don't do their fair share. We get angry and find it hard to celebrate with others because we don't feel celebrated ourselves. And resentment and lack of joy make our hearts grow hard. We find that doing the work of God is destroying the work of God in us.

The bad news is no matter how often you come to church or how many ministries you serve, once resentment and lack of joy characterize your life, you become as far from God as the younger brother.

The good news is the father is running out to you to welcome you home as well. When the older son refused to come in, the father ran out to him, just as he did the younger son. And he said,

> "My son, you are always with me, and everything I have is yours. But we had to celebrate and be glad because this brother of yours was dead and is alive again; he was lost and is found."

You see, the father loves both sons the same. He runs out to meet the younger son. He runs out to meet the older son. He welcomes both. He celebrates both. Jesus leaves the story open-ended. We are not told whether the older son came inside or not.

I said it earlier, and I believe it to be true; it is often easier for the younger son to go back to his father than it is for the older son. The journey for the younger son begins with forgiveness. So does the journey for the older son.

It begins with asking God to forgive us for being at home with him all along and not experiencing the joy of it. Forgiveness for envying the life of our younger brothers and sisters while ignoring the life God has offered us in God's presence. Forgiveness for seeing our service to God as duty instead of an honor. Sometimes the older brother comes out in me. I find myself dreading the task of preparing another message for yet another Sunday. Sundays seem to roll around with amazing regularity. Then I am reminded that to teach the Scripture is an incredible honor. One of which I am not worthy. Then it is no longer a task. It becomes a privilege.

After forgiveness, the next step is learning to live in gratitude. All of life is a gift, but for some reason, we forget that, and we think we are owed something. Then we begin to resent what others have. But, gratitude drives away resentment. The two cannot exist side by side.

G. K. Chesterton once wrote, "Here ends another day during which I have had eyes, ears, hands and the great world around me, and tomorrow begins another. Why am I allowed two?"[24] Life is a gift.

Maybe we should all make a list and go over it first thing every morning to remind us of all we have to be grateful for. A man named John Ortberg made such a list. Here is his list;

> I was made in the image of God. I have a body,
> and most of it works. I have eyes that see and
> feet that walk. Many people don't. Yet that's
> what I have each day.

---

[24] *G. K. Chesterton, quoted by John Ortberg, Love Beyond Reason, p.106.*

God loves me. He calls me his child. Because Jesus came to teach and live, died on a cross, and was resurrected—I have a future assured with God forever.

I have been received into God's ultimate dream: the new community. I'm part of the church. I belong—I can be loved and accepted.

I have been gifted, created to make a unique, eternal contribution to the work of God. I have a calling. Even when I foul up, God promises to work through me in spite of my mistakes.[25]

That's a pretty good list. As a child of God, we have no reason to resent any other child of God, especially not the wayward ones. Because they are missing out on the joy we can know each and every day.

And the final step home is understanding that you are loved by your heavenly parent every bit as much as any younger son or daughter. The father loves both sons. He ran out to meet both sons, and he welcomes both sons to the party. He wants both sons to really know his presence and experience his joy.

I have a word for all of the older sons and daughters. On the outside, you do everything just right. You act the way good Christians should. But, on the inside, there is resentment, anger, and a lack of joy. Listen. God loves you more than you know. God also pleads with you to come home. Find the joy God wants you to have.

If you are the younger son or daughter, the way home is through forgiveness and a willingness to change.

If you are an older son or daughter, the way home is through forgiveness, gratitude, and knowing you are loved.

---

[25] *Ortberg. Ibid. p.108.*

No matter which kind of son or daughter you have turned out to be, God is head over heels in love with you, and God welcomes you home.

§

The Story of Two Sons And Their Father:
Part III (Luke 15)

Becoming Like The Father

This is not just the story of the younger son. It is also the story of the older son. It is the story of two sons. But, it is also the story of a father. And now, that is the character we will focus on, the father.

The father is a prominent figure in Rembrandt's portrait to which we have been referring. In the painting, he is old, partially blind. The most outstanding characteristics you see are his face and hands. It is the face of an old father. A face that has known the joys and heartaches of parenthood. A face that has laughed and cried and spent many a night awake. It is a face that has known unspeakable joy and sorrow.

Let's hear this story one more time and this time look at the parts of the story that describe the actions of the father. Remember, the younger son took his share of the estate and went away and squandered it. He lived for himself and thumbed his nose at the things his father held dear. But, when things didn't work out, and he found himself broke and alone, he returned home.

> *But while he was still a long way off, his father saw him and was filled with compassion for him; he ran to his son, threw his arms around him, and kissed him.*[26] *The son said to him, "Father, I have sinned against heaven and against you. I am no longer worthy to be called your*

---

[26] *Actually, the verb tense in the Greek language indicates continuous action, i.e., He just kept kissing him.*

son." But the father said to his servants, "Quick! Bring the best robe and put it on him. Put a ring on his finger and sandals on his feet. Bring the fattened calf and kill it. Let's have a feast and celebrate. For this son of mine was dead and is alive again; he was lost and is found." So they began to celebrate.

And when the elder son refused to come into the house and join the celebration, the father went out to him and said, *"My son, you are always with me, and everything I have is yours."* (Luke 15:31)

Look at some of the characteristics of the father.

1. The father loves lavishly.

When the younger son comes home, he does not find a father sitting smugly in his recliner, saying, "So, you came back? How did that whole 'give me my part of the inheritance now' work out for you?" Instead, he found a father so overjoyed at his return that nothing he had done mattered anymore. In the father's own words, "We had given you up for dead. But here you are alive. Let's celebrate!" And with that, the younger son was welcomed back into the family with grace and joy.

"Quick," the father says, "get his robe and ring and sandals." Quick. There is no waiting period to see if he really has changed. No. His willingness to come home was change enough to get started. He was welcomed back immediately. Of course, that is how God welcomes us back. Immediately, as soon as we make the effort to return, God grants us a place in his kingdom as his sons and daughters. No waiting. No trial period. In one of Thomas Merton's prayers he writes,

> *"My Lord God, I have no idea where I am going. I do not see the road ahead of me. I cannot know for certain*

where it will end. Nor do I really know myself, and the fact that I think that I am following your will does not mean that I am actually doing so. But I believe that the desire to please you does, in fact, please you.'[27]

That's where it starts, with the desire to please God. And that is enough to get started.

The younger son is given a robe. The robe is a sign of his sonship. The ring is the family ring, another sign that he is welcomed completely back into the family. The shoes are a symbol of sonship too. Slaves were barefoot. Servants were barefoot. The family members had shoes. Shoes meant you were family.

And then the father gave him a party. He was so happy he had returned. He had to share the good news with everyone. This image is especially meaningful to me. To think that God is so excited that every time a child comes home that God throws a party in his or her honor. You come home, and God reaches for the banners and confetti. That is how important we are to God.

To the older son, the father says, "Everything I have is yours." And it appears the father has a lot. This is no poor old farmer. With all of the servants and land, this father appears to be a wealthy landowner. Even after his son squandered a large part of his estate, he still has plenty. And everything he has is available to his children. All of it. This father is generous and gracious. Here Jesus paints a picture for us of God. God is generous and gracious to us. God doesn't merely mete out to us our due. God runs to us and abundantly lavishes love on us.

2. He never compares his two sons.[28]

While the father celebrates the return of the younger son, he never neglects the older. While he welcomes home the younger son, he also

---

[27] *Thomas Merton, from Thoughts In Solitude, www.onbeing.org*
[28] *Henri Nouwen, Ibid. pp.102-105.*

welcomes home the older. He doesn't compare and weigh them against each other.

This may be one of the most incredible things about God. Like this father, our heavenly parent doesn't compare children. God doesn't love any one of us more than another. Henri Nouwen writes, "I cannot fathom how all of God's children can be favorites. And still, they are."[29]

That is hard of us to hear because we are so into comparing. We live in a world where everything is a competition, a comparison. We are more or less attractive, more or less intelligent, more or less successful than somebody else. We don't know how to react to God who loves us all the same. The elder brother started comparing himself to the younger brother and became jealous and envious. When we compare ourselves with others, it always leads to jealousy or envy or a sense of self-importance and arrogance. But, God doesn't compare us. God just loves us. The joy that would be ours if we could just learn to stop comparing and competing with each other.

Jesus told a story about some workers in a vineyard and the landowner which I think still confuses people. (Matthew 20:1-16) He said the kingdom of heaven is like a man who owned a vineyard and went out and hired some laborers early in the morning. They agreed on a fair wage for a day's work. Later in the day, he went out and got some more workers, and then near the end of the day, he hired some more. When the day was over, he paid those workers who came at the end of the day first. He paid those who came in the middle of the day the same amount he had agreed to pay those who had worked all day. Then he also paid those who came at the end of the day the same amount he had agreed to pay those who worked all day. When those who worked all day saw that those who had only worked half a day or just a few hours got paid as much as they did, they were angry. The landowner asked them why they were angry. They got paid a fair wage, a wage they had agreed upon. If no one else had been hired

[29] Ibid.

and they had been paid that wage at the end of the day, they would have been happy about it. But, they were angry because they were comparing themselves and their work with others, who they felt were not as deserving as they were.

It never occurred to them, nor does it seem to occur to us that the landowner wanted those who worked all day to rejoice in his generosity toward those who had worked less. They were happy with their wages until they started comparing. Once they started comparing, they became bitter. But, in God's way of thinking, those who have done little are loved as much as those who have done much. The parable ends with the landowner saying,

> *"Friend, I am not being unfair to you. Didn't you agree to work for a denarius? Take your pay and go. I want to give the man who was hired last the same as I gave you. Don't I have the right to do what I want with my own money? Or are you envious because I am generous?"*

It is the same thing as saying, "My child, you are always with me, and everything I have is yours. Why are you bitter because I celebrate your brother?"

God is not just the landowner to us, but our loving, heavenly parent. God loves us all the same. We are all God's favorites. God doesn't compare. There is joy waiting for us when we learn to stop comparing ourselves to others.

In this story that Jesus told, we understand that the father in the story represents God. God is the one who is compassionate, merciful, and forgiving. But doesn't the Bible say that we are supposed to behave like God? We are not gods, we will never be gods, but we are called to act like the God who created us. We are supposed to act like Jesus who is the image of God. We easily identify with the younger son or the older son, but what if the goal of this story is for us to identify with the father?

At some point in life, a strange thing happens. One day you look in the mirror, and the face that stares back at you surprises you. It is no longer the face of the young man or young woman you always thought you would be. Instead, it is a face that looks much more like your father's face or your mother's face. Somewhere along the way, you stopped being just the son or daughter; you became the parent.

And just as it happens in our physical lives, it should also happen in our spiritual lives. Our goal is to grow up and no longer be a wayward or bitter child but to become like the father. The father in this story is merciful. And Jesus said, "Be merciful, just as your Father is merciful." (Luke 6:36)

When we talk about this story, we talk so much about, "Which son are you?" But, the real question is, "Are you interested in becoming like the father?" Are you ready to not just accept forgiveness but to be the one who offers forgiveness to those who have wronged you? Are you ready to not just be welcomed home, but are you ready to welcome others home? Are you ready to not just be the one who receives compassion, but are you ready to show compassion to others?

We live in a society that encourages us to remain dependent children. To live for self-gratification. To indulge our selfish desires. But, the joy comes from growing up. The joy comes when we stop being the younger son or daughter and become the father.

Too many Christians I have met think they can remain younger sons their whole lives. They can just keep wandering away and coming back when things don't work out. They keep living self-centered lives. After all of these years, they still think it is "all about me." But, there comes a time when all younger sons and daughters must leave "Never-Never Land" and grow up. There comes a time when we must realize that life is not just about our having been forgiven. It is also about forgiving others. It is about helping others find forgiveness too. There comes a time when we have to stop being the younger son and become the father.

Too many Christians remain the older brother their whole lives. They continue to serve out of duty and obligation. They are judgmental and resentful. They are always comparing themselves to others. They think they must compete for God's love. But, there comes a time when older sons and daughters must grow up. There comes a time when we must realize that life is not about us but about celebrating the lives of others. There is a time when we stop being the older brother and become the father.

The Apostle Paul wrote these words,

> *"When I was a child, I talked like a child, I thought like a child, I reasoned like a child. When I became man, I put childish ways behind me."* (1 Corinthians 13:11)

If I may paraphrase: When I was the younger son, I talked like the younger son, I thought like the younger son, I reasoned like the younger son. When I became like the father, I put the younger son's ways behind me.

When I was the older son, I talked like the older son, I thought like the older son, I reasoned like the older son. When I became like the father, I put the older son's ways behind me.

As we have examined this story, you may have identified most with the younger son, or you may have identified most with the older son. It doesn't really matter. The good news is that you can become like the father. Actually, that is the goal. What a joyful day it will be when you and I look into the mirror, and the life that stares back at us looks more like our heavenly parent than the sons and daughters we used to be. Let it be soon, dear God. Let it be soon.

§

Living In the Light

Those of us who are followers of Jesus believe that we can live with hope. The main reason for this, of course, is the resurrection of Jesus, celebrated by many as Easter. Many in less liturgical traditions are unaware that Easter is not just a single day but a season in the Christian year. It lasts from Easter Sunday until Pentecost.

It is a fifty-day celebration that reminds us that Easter and resurrection living is for the entire year, not just one day. In the Scripture, even those who live in the light of the resurrection have to learn to do so. It doesn't come naturally.

From them we learn about the struggle of learning to live in the light of the resurrection. We also learn to live with joy. I hope the light of their stories will shed light on our own stories as we learn to live in hope.

§

Seeing Is Believing (John 9)

This story is 41 verses long, an entire chapter divided into seven sections. We'll begin, logically enough, at the beginning.

Section 1: A person, Not A Topic.

We are never given the name of this blind man. He is simply referred to as "the blind man." There will be a lot of wordplay and double meaning throughout this story around the words "See" and "Blind." For instance, the Bible says that as Jesus went along, he *saw* this blind man. The disciples noticed that he was there, but they didn't really *see* him.

Most likely, he was sitting by the street with a container of some kind hoping people would put money in it because he had no way to support himself. When the disciples noticed him sitting there, they wanted to discuss theology. They asked Jesus why was he blind. Was it because of some sin he had committed or something his parents had done? They didn't *see* a blind man. They saw a topic for discussion. And by the way, why is it necessary to blame people who are already vulnerable? Why do we insist on doing that?

Jesus, on the other hand, *saw* a human being, created and loved by God, who had a need.

Jesus shot a hole in their theology and basically told them he wasn't going to sit around and discuss theological conspiracy theories with them. They could save those for Facebook! Jesus *saw* a person, not a topic.

This very first scene is a little unnerving to me because it reminds me of how much like the Duh-ciples we can be sometimes. We spend too much time discussing things like racism and poverty and the health care crisis in our country, but we do little about it on a corporate or societal scale. Over six hundred thousand people have died in the United States of COVID-19 at the time of this writing, and the dying hasn't stopped yet. Unless one of the casualties happened to be Aunt Joan, they remain just faceless statistics to us. Over half a million people and so many still don't really *see* them.

Jesus *saw* this man, and because he *saw* him, he reached out to do something about his situation. Jesus spat on the ground (but not for the same reason some folks spit on the ground). He made mud with the spit and clay and put it on the blind man's eyes. Then he told him to go and wash it off.

The blind man did as he was told, and when he washed it off, he could see for the first time in his life. He could see! Excited, he went home to tell everybody.

Section Two: Gossip Over The Fence. (Which, by the way, is the longest section in the Book of John in which Jesus is not present.)

When the blind man, no longer blind, got home, the gossip over the backyard fences started flying. The neighbors saw him running around and yelling that he could see. They were asking, "Hey isn't that the blind guy next door?" Some said it was. Others said it wasn't; it was just a guy who looked like him. We know he never saw his neighbors. It appears they never *saw* him either. They couldn't even recognize him. So, he tells them what happened.

He said he didn't know what the man looked like. He didn't see him. But, look at who he calls Jesus. He calls him a man. Watch how his faith in who Jesus is grows throughout this story.

Section Three: The Interrogation

The Pharisees caught wind of what had happened, and they were upset. It appears that Jesus healed this man on the Sabbath, which violated the Pharisee's understanding of the Law. Can you imagine being blind your whole life, and then finally you get healed, but on the wrong day! They dragged the man in for questioning. He told them what he had experienced; he had been blind, now he could *see!*

Notice this man's faith. First, Jesus was just a man, now he believes Jesus must be a prophet.

Section Four: Just The Facts, Ma'am.

It was obvious the man could now see. It is amazing how we try to deny things that do not fit our tribal narratives, isn't it? The neighbors did not want to believe that he had been healed. So, some of them tried to say he was a different person than the one who had been blind. The Pharisees didn't want to admit that he had been healed, so they insinuated that he was never really blind in the first place. He had just been running into things all those years for sympathy. People still do the same thing. When confronted with theological facts, scientific facts, political facts that don't match what we want to believe, we make up stories that fit our tribal narratives and choose to believe them instead of the truth.

So, now, the Pharisees call in his parents for questioning.

Their theological narrative did not allow for someone who was born blind to be able to see. Since this man could obviously see, then they questioned whether or not he was really born blind. But, his parents said, "Listen, this is our son, and he was born blind."

There are three questions the Pharisees kept asking:

        1) Was this guy really blind?

        2) If he was blind, how is it that now he can see?

        3) Who is the man who healed him?

They only asked the parents the first two questions. Was he born blind, and can he see now? But the parents answered all three questions. They said, yes, he was born blind, yes, he can now see, but we don't know who did it. Well, of course, they knew. He had told them.

But, they didn't want to get into trouble. They answered a question they were not even asked just to stay out of trouble.

It is like when you are talking with your child, and you ask her, "Have you been playing in Mom and Dad's bedroom?" And she answers, "No, I haven't been in there, and I don't know anything about the broken lamp either!" Guilty people often answer questions they aren't asked.

In order to get off of the hot seat, his parents told them, "Hey, our son is an adult; ask him these questions." There is nothing like getting thrown under the bus by your own parents!

Section Five: The Interrogation—The Sequel.

"Hey man, I am no theologian. I don't know all of the rules you have about what God is supposed to be like. I just know that I was blind, and now I can see."

But, they were not deterred by the truth. They started asking the same questions over and over again. Question the truth long enough and loud enough, and maybe people will stop believing the truth.

The man who had been healed had had enough. It was all really starting to get old to him. He had been blind his entire life, and the last thing he wanted to do was sit inside this stuffy room filled with stuffy people and repeat the same answers to the same questions over and over. He wanted to go outside and see the flowers he could only smell before. He had heard birds singing, and now he wanted to go outside and watch them fly. There was a woman who always spoke kindly to him as he heard the clink of coins she was dropping into his cup. He wanted to find her and look into her face. He didn't have time for this. He had been blind his whole life. Now he was beginning to wonder if these guys had all gone deaf![30] They couldn't hear the simple truth.

Finally, he asked, "Why do you want to know so much about him? Do you want to be his disciples too?" I believe he knew that would

---

[30] *Paul Duke, Irony In The Fourth Gospel, p.121.*

end the questioning. And it did. They got angry. Called him names. He got a little sarcastic with them.

After that, they threw him out. Out of the room. Out of the synagogue. At first, the healed man said Jesus was man, then he said he was a prophet, and now, he says he must be from God.

Section Six: A Friend On The Outside.

When they threw him out, guess who looked him up?

He didn't recognize Jesus because he had never seen him before. When Jesus asked him if he had faith in him, the man answered, "Lord, I believe." And he worshiped him. Notice the progression of the man's faith. He told his neighbors that Jesus was a man. He told the Pharisees that Jesus was a prophet. At the second interrogation, he told the Pharisees that Jesus was sent from God. Finally, when he *saw* Jesus, he called him Lord and worshiped him. His faith was complete. Not only was he healed physically. Now he could really *see* the truth.

Section Seven: (The final section.) Blind In The Worst Way.

Earlier Jesus said, "I am the Light of the World." Then he healed this blind man as a sign of how he came to bring sight and light to those of us who live in the darkness of our own sins and prejudices.

This man was born physically blind. The Pharisees could see; physically, they possessed sight. But, in everything else that matters, they were blind. After meeting Jesus, this man could now see; his eyes were opened both physically and in other ways. The Pharisees were still blind. They were blind because they could not open their eyes and their lives to the "Light of the World." They chose instead to live in darkness.

This story reminds me of a quote by one of my heroes, a fellow Alabamian, Helen Keller. Helen Keller was born blind and deaf. Yet she wrote, "There are none so blind as those who will not see."[31]

---

[31] *Helen Keller, quotes.net.*

Helen Keller was one of those people without physical sight who *saw* the world more clearly than many sighted people.

Jesus is the light of the world who came to save us from our darkness and our blindness, not just our sin.

Let me give you a personal example. When I was writing this, I was overwhelmed by the news and the video of the murder of Ahmaud Arbery. It is the result of decades of either embracing or ignoring racism and white supremacy in the south and throughout our entire nation. Racism and white supremacy are a darkness into which I was born. It was the culture in which I grew up. It was the darkness in which I learned to walk. Since my skin is white, I was blind to the darkness in which I lived.

I thank God for the writings of Holy Scripture and Harper Lee and James Cone, and others who shined light into my darkness and helped me to see. The Light of the World not only forgave me of my personal sins but gave me sight so that I might learn to see the world as God sees the world. So that I might change the way I think and live. You cannot follow Jesus and choose to live in darkness. If we truly *see*, it changes the way we live.

John Newton wrote those famous, beloved words:

Amazing Grace, how sweet the sound
That saved a wretch, like me
I once was lost, but now I'm found
Was blind, but now I see.

In those words, he speaks of his own forgiveness, but he also speaks of how God opened his eyes. He wasn't just forgiven of his personal sin. John Newton quit the slave trade business. He once was blind, but now he could see. His new sight changed his life.

Racism is not the only darkness we live in. It is just one of many. But, Isaiah and Matthew both encourage us to realize that even though we are a people living in darkness, we have seen a great light.

Even though we live in the land of the shadow of death, a light has dawned.[32]

We no longer have to live in darkness because Jesus came and shined a light so that we can *see* the world as God sees the world.

The Covid pandemic did not break our culture or even our economy. It merely exposed the cracks and chasms that were already there. We have lived with them by choosing not to *see* them. We have lived in blindness, ignoring, for instance, the fact that we live in the richest nation in the world and over half of our citizens could not afford an unexpected expense of more than $400. We have been blind to the wealth injustice all around us. We can go back to living in the darkness, or we can go through the painful work of adjusting our eyes to the light of a new way of seeing the world.

When we live in darkness, we live in self-righteousness and hate and selfishness. When we live in light, we see people as God sees people. In the light, people are no longer black and white, male and female, rich and poor, essential and non-essential, expendable and non- expendable, straight and gay. We see people as the children of God, and we treat them like sisters and brothers. I have it on good word that one day this darkness will end.

Hear the Good News: Jesus is the Light of the World. We can choose to leave our darkness and walk in the Light.

§

---

[32] *Isaiah 9:2; Matthew 4:16*

Faces of Easter (John 20:1-8; 11-16; 24-28; 31)

Let's talk about Easter! It is the Holiest day of the year for those of us who are followers of Jesus Christ. This is the day that marks his resurrection from the dead. The day that God authenticated who Jesus was and the life that he lived. It is a great day!

Some of you don't quite believe in the resurrection. Then some of you don't quite believe in the resurrection, but you would like to! God knows it is hard enough to get through life all by yourself. It would be great if you could believe that there is a God who loves you.

Some of you are hoping that something will happen that will help you believe.

We come to Easter feeling a lot of different things. Our days may be more like the first Easter morning than you have imagined. Waking up with the sorrow and grief from the day before still with us. Hearing news that just seems too good to be true. Trapped between the present reality and hope.

Let's look at some of the people on that first Easter morning and see their faith or lack of faith. Let's look into their eyes and see the faces of Easter.

The first two faces we are going to look at are the faces of Peter and John.

On Friday, Jesus was crucified. His dead body was taken down off of the cross and buried in a nearby tomb. It was almost Sabbath, so there was no time to go through the proper burial and anointing. So, they laid the body in the tomb and sealed it. They intended to come back at the end of the Sabbath and anoint the body with oils and spices and prepare a proper burial.

The women went early on Sunday morning to do their job. But when they arrived, the stone at the entrance of the tomb had been moved, and the body was gone. They did not know what to make of it. They ran back to where the disciples were hiding out together. They told the disciples that someone had stolen the body. They did not believe in a resurrection, just a robbery.

Peter and John ran to the tomb to see for themselves. There is a lot of running going on that first Easter. John refers to himself as the "other disciple." Often as the "other disciple, the one whom Jesus loved," which sounds kind of privileged, but you can do that if you write the book.

JOHN

The Scripture says that John outran Peter and got there first. Remember John wrote this. He likes for everyone to know that he could outrun Peter. When John got to the tomb, he looked inside and saw the linens lying there, but he did not go inside. Then, finally, he says, Peter got there. Now he is just rubbing it in. Peter walked past John into the tomb and looked at the linens and the cloth that had been wrapped around Jesus' head. They were lying there perfectly wrapped as if there was a body in them, but the body was gone.

At that point, the other disciple, John, the one who reached the tomb first, (he adds one more time), looks around, and the Scripture says, "He saw and believed." Just like that. He didn't see the resurrected Christ. All he saw was an empty tomb, and that was enough. He believed that Jesus was alive.

I have met people like John. They can't really remember a time when they did not believe. They have gone to church their entire lives, plus the nine months before they were born. They have believed in Jesus from the time they first heard about him. Not to have faith in God and not know his presence is foreign to them. The

Gospel makes perfect sense to them. How could anyone not believe? I envy people like that. I envy John. Faith comes so easy to him. Belief seems so natural to him.

There are a lot of people like John. The first time they heard the Gospel, they became followers of Jesus. They don't need a lot of evidence. They just know it's true. Some of you are like John.

PETER

Peter is a different story. He looked around inside that empty tomb and saw the same things John saw. But Peter didn't leave believing. Peter left confused. He saw the same things John saw, but it didn't lead him to believe. Why do two people hear the Gospel, and one of them believes, and the other doesn't? It has always been that way. John believed. At the time, Peter did not believe that Jesus was alive.

Maybe it was because he felt guilty. Maybe that is why John beat him to the tomb. According to the old song, "guilty feet ain't got no rhythm." The last time he saw Jesus was in the courtyard of the High Priest. They were taking Jesus inside, where they beat him and made fun of him, and finalized their plan to kill him. There in the courtyard, Peter was recognized. They wanted to know if he was with Jesus. "NO!" he said. Three times he said it. A rooster crowed, and he ran out of there as fast as he could. He found a dark, quiet place, and he wept. He wept for Jesus. He wept for himself. He wasn't sure what to think. If Jesus was alive, Peter wasn't so sure he wanted to see him. Not after what he had done. Even if it was real, how could it mean anything for him? He had had his chance and blown it.

I have met people like Peter. A part of them want to believe, but they just can't. Sometimes it is out of guilt. "If Jesus is alive, I'm not sure I want to see him after what I have done." When we can't forgive ourselves, it's is hard to believe that God can forgive us.

Of course, later on, Peter did become a believer. It took more than it took for John. Peter had to see the risen Christ and hear his words of forgiveness, words he offered to Peter and to everyone following in Peter's footsteps down through the centuries.

Some of you are like Peter. You are just not sure that you are the kind of person who fits into this religious thing. You are just not sure God really loves you and accepts you. You have never considered something like this was within your realm of possibility.

MARY

The next face is the face of Mary

After Peter and John left, Mary went back to the tomb by herself. She looked inside, and this time there were two angels or messengers sitting there. She was crying.

"Why are you crying?"

"Someone has taken his body, and I don't know where they have taken it."

Then she turned and saw a man standing there. It was Jesus, but she didn't recognize him. Some people think it is strange that she didn't recognize him. But I think I understand. It is hard to recognize God sometimes when you have tears in your eyes. Tears and tragedies have a way of blinding us to the sight of God right there in front of us.

I have met people like Mary. They experience a tragedy or difficult time in life, and they don't believe God is there. They don't believe in this whole resurrection thing because if God were real, they wouldn't have had to go through what they were going through. I have met people who couldn't see God for their own tears. And the whole time, God was standing right there in front of them.

She asked, "Do you know where they have taken the body?" And Jesus replied, "Mary." That is all he said. "Mary." She turned to him and recognized who he was. She believed. She saw him. She knew he was alive. Sometimes God is hard to see in our lives. But, if we listen, he often finds ways of calling our name. Ways that we can hear and understand. What is more life-changing than knowing that the God who created everything knows your name?

Some of you are like Mary. You have been through a lot of hard times, and you have always thought that meant there was no God. If Jesus were real, where was he when you needed him? Like Mary, God has been with you the whole time. It is just hard to see God when your eyes are blurred by tears.

THOMAS

The last face is the face of Thomas. Thomas heard the rumors that Jesus was alive. Some of his very best friends believed it. But, not Thomas. This was just too far-fetched. "When you are dead, you are dead." "Let's just face the facts, people, and get on with our lives."

I have met people like Thomas. People who just find it hard to believe, some on intellectual grounds.

"I would like to believe if I could, but I have high SAT scores." The world is full of misery and death. And a lot of the people who claim to be followers of God are a big part of the problem. There are plenty of reasons to scoff.

Jesus appeared before Thomas and told him to go ahead, to touch his hands and his side if he needed to. At that point, Thomas didn't need to. He said, "My Lord and my God." It still didn't make sense. I don't believe all of Thomas' doubts automatically went away. But it was enough. He saw Jesus in a way that was enough for him. And it still happens that way. Believing doesn't mean you understand it all, and it doesn't mean that it always makes sense. It doesn't mean you won't have any more doubts. It does mean that—in some way—you have experienced God's presence, and it is enough to sustain your faith, doubts and all.

Some of you are like Thomas. You have never been big on religion. What you have read in the Bible about Jesus and what you have seen in the lives of a lot of Christians doesn't even seem to be remotely related. It is okay to have questions. It is okay to have doubts. But, if you are open to the possibility that there is a God who created everything and that God loves you, that may be enough. Enough to sustain faith, even with your doubts.

It is not about believing everything at once. It is about being open to mystery. Being open to the possibility of things you haven't figured out and may never figure out. We can't know and we can't prove everything. God welcomes you, doubts and all.

There are four faces of Easter that John shows us. John, who found it easy to believe. Peter who wanted to believe, but took a while to understand that his guilt could be removed and that God still loved him. Mary, who in a time of great heartache, heard Jesus call her name. And Thomas, the old doubter, who was faced with a love so great it won over his entire heart, if not his entire mind.

My guess is one of these faces is your face, that you identify with at least one of these people. Or maybe you feel like you have identified with all of them.

At the end of this chapter, John wrote: *"But these are written that you may believe that Jesus is the Messiah, the Son of God, and that by believing you may have life in his name."*

That is my hope and prayer for you: that you may believe that Jesus is the Messiah, that he is the Son of God, that he is alive and present with us today. The point is that John and Peter and Mary and Thomas all came to believe from a different place, a different perspective. But, they all came to believe. We are not all the same. We come to God from different places. No matter who you are, no matter what you have done, no matter what you have been through, no matter how great your doubts, I pray that the risen Christ will make himself known to you that you might believe and by believing, find life in his name.

§

Breakfast in Galilee John 21:1-19

Let's take a closer look at what happened after that first Easter Sunday. John tells us in his Gospel that Jesus first appeared to the women at the tomb. Later, he appeared to the disciples in the room where they were hiding. Most of the disciples were there. Thomas, however, was not. We are not told where he was. He just wasn't there. When they told Thomas that Jesus had appeared to them, he did not believe them. He said, *"Unless I see the nail marks in his hands and put my finger where the nails were, and put my hand into his side, I will not believe."*

Later Jesus appeared to the disciples again. This time Thomas was with them. Jesus took Thomas up on his request. Jesus said to Thomas, *"Put your finger here; see my hands. Reach out your hand and put it into my side. Stop doubting and believe."* Of course, after Jesus called him on it, he didn't have to actually touch the wounds. Seeing was enough.

After Jesus appeared to Thomas, Thomas did believe. Then Jesus spoke these words, *"Because you have seen me, you have believed; blessed are those who have not seen and yet have believed."*

That word was not for Thomas. That word was for us. It is as if we are watching the scene and Jesus is talking to Thomas. Then he turns to the camera and winks at us as he speaks those words. Because we are the ones who haven't seen and yet believe. We were not there. We did not see the risen Christ, not physically. Jesus wanted us to know that we are blessed for believing without seeing.

So, Jesus had appeared to his disciples after the crucifixion and burial. He appeared to them, and they knew he was alive. They experienced the first Easter ever. They saw him standing in front of them, talking to them. They knew he was alive. They had the best Easter service ever! So, what did they do the next week?

Well, Peter said, "I'm going fishing." That is unexpected. Jesus has risen from the dead. Now what? Well, I think I will go fishing. Now I am sure a lot of folks go fishing on Sunday, the week after Easter, but this was Peter! He is one of the main disciples. He goes fishing. The others decide to follow along with him.

But they weren't catching anything. Have you ever noticed how often the Bible says they were out fishing, but they weren't catching anything? It makes you wonder how they stayed in business sometimes. They were fishing at night. The sun came up. They still had not caught anything.

They saw someone on the shore. He called out to them and asked if they had caught any fish. "No," they shouted back. He said, "Try fishing on the right side of the boat." Apparently, they were fishing on the wrong side of the boat! So, they did what he said. They were unable to haul in all of the fish they caught in that cast. They remembered that this had happened before. The last time it happened, it was Jesus who told them to cast on the right side of the boat. They had just seen Jesus and knew he had risen from the dead. So, they figured this guy must be Jesus. As a matter of fact, the disciple referred to as "the one Jesus loved" turned to Peter and said, "It is the Lord."

Then Peter, who had apparently gone commando while they were fishing on the boat, put his outer garment back on and jumped into the water and swam to shore while the others made their way in the boat. When they arrived at the shore, Jesus was waiting on them. He had a fire going. There is something interesting about the fire. John tells us it was a charcoal fire.

That phrase is only used one other time in the Bible to describe a fire. It is used to describe the fire outside the place where Jesus had been taken after they arrested him in the Garden of Gethsemane. It was the fire Peter stood near to warm himself. It was the fire where Peter denied three times that he knew Jesus. Here around the same kind of fire, Jesus will give Peter three opportunities to reaffirm his commitment to him.

Jesus cooked some fish. They ate breakfast in Galilee together. The Scripture says they all knew it was the Lord.

There are several themes in this story that we find in other stories. I mentioned earlier that the disciples had a hard time catching any fish that night until Jesus told them to cast on the right side of the boat. As a matter of fact, the disciples never catch a fish in any of the Gospels without Jesus' help.[33] I think that is meant to speak to us on a different level. You remember, Jesus told them that he was going to make them fishers of people. I think it was a way of reminding them and us that we will not bring anyone into the kingdom without Jesus. Without the prevenient grace of God going before us, we cannot bring people into God's kingdom. If we want to see people come to have a relationship with God, it will not happen through our proclamations and rules. They must see Jesus. They must see Jesus in us.

Another theme, of course, is their confusion over his identity. At first, they were not sure who he was. Like Mary who, when she saw him after the resurrection, thought at first that he was the gardener. Mary may not have been far off when you think about it. The Bible says that Jesus is the new Adam. What was Adam? He was a gardener.[34]

Maybe those stories are to remind us that Jesus is still present with us, but we do not recognize him. I think there is a lot of truth to that. I think God is at work all around us, and we fail to recognize God's presence. Maybe, the reason those stories are there is to remind us that it has always been that way.

But, the thing that I find really interesting is the meal. Jesus prepared a breakfast of fish and bread for them. And they all ate it together.

On the Thursday evening before Jesus was arrested, they ate the Passover together. That was when Jesus told them that when they ate

[33] Thomas H. Troeger, *Feasting on the Word*, "Homilitical Perspective" p.423.

[34] Len Sweet, conversation with Fresh Expressions Team. Feb. 9, 2019.

the bread to remember his body given for them and when they drank the wine to remember his blood shed for them. He turned the Passover Meal into what we now celebrate as the Lord's Supper.

We sometimes call it the Last Supper because it is the last meal Jesus ate with his disciples before he was crucified. But, it wasn't the last meal. After his resurrection, Jesus ate several more meals with them. Here they are, eating breakfast together in Galilee.

Maybe, it is a reminder to us that the Passover Meal was not the last meal that Jesus would eat with his disciples. Maybe, it is to remind us that Jesus continues to meet us in the meal some of us call Holy Communion.

On the road to Emmaus, Jesus was walking with two disciples, and they were talking about all the things that had happened in Jerusalem. They did not recognize Jesus and were telling him about how Jesus had been crucified, and now some were saying that he was alive. It was not until they stopped and had a meal together that they recognized him. It was when he broke the bread that they realized who he was.

And so it is with us. Jesus makes himself known to us when we come to his table. The Gospels are not just stories about things that happened long ago. They are stories about how God is with us now. They are stories about how God makes himself known to us today. They are stories about how slow we are to recognize God when it does happen.

Jesus is still not through sharing meals with his disciples. He meets us at his table. Some call it Mass. Some call it Eucharist. Some call it Holy Communion. Some call it the Lord's Supper. Whatever we call it, in the breaking of bread and drinking from the cup, we will recognize his presence with us.

§

What I Would Give For A Power-Hungry Church (Acts 1:1-8)

There was a First United Methodist Church that was very staid and formal in the way they worshipped. One day a man was visiting their church. He was from a Pentecostal background, and during the sermon, the pastor said something the visitor really liked.

"Hallelujah! Amen, brother," the man shouted.

Well, this kind of thing wasn't done in the worship services at this church. An usher walked over to where he was sitting, and he said, "Sir, we don't do that here. It disturbs others."

The man apologized and said, "Oh, I am so sorry. I didn't know. It just sort of slipped out."

A little later, the pastor said something else the man really liked, and he amenned him again. Once again, the usher went over to him and said, "Sir, I told you we don't do that here, and if you have another outburst, I will have to ask you to leave." The man apologized again.

But, soon, the pastor said something else the man liked, and he shouted again. The usher went over to him and said, "Sir, I am going to have to ask you to leave now."

The man said, "I am so sorry. I can't help it. I've just got the Spirit."

The usher said, "Yes, I can tell you have got the Spirit, but I assure you, you didn't get it here!"

In a very real way, this story speaks to the contrast between church today and the season we are celebrating.

The Ascension of Jesus is ten days before Pentecost. Jesus spoke to his disciples right before he ascended into heaven.

He spoke to them about the Holy Spirit. He explained that he was leaving. He would no longer be physically present with them. The Holy Spirit would be with them. The Holy Spirit would continue Jesus' work in and through them. He told them to wait in Jerusalem. Soon the Holy Spirit would come and give them guidance.

Ten days later—on the day of Pentecost—that promise was fulfilled.

Let's take a look at the promise Jesus made and what it meant for them and for us.

Jesus was actually repeating a promise that had been made by John the Baptist way back in Luke 3:16-17:

"John answered them all, 'I baptize you with water. But one who is more powerful than I will come, the straps of whose sandals I am not worthy to untie. He will baptize you with the Holy Spirit and with fire.'"

Jesus told them when the Holy Spirit came, they would receive power. Power. The disciples didn't really know what to do with that word. They were not used to having power. They weren't sure what Jesus meant.

At first, they thought he must be talking about political power. They could use some of that. They were tired of being at the mercy of the Romans. They were tired of having their religious beliefs and practices monitored by Roman Law. Their first response was to ask Jesus if he was talking about political power. We always seem to think that is the way the church needs to get things done. Yet, history serves as a warning to us. Every time the church has gotten political power, it has never turned out so well for the church or anyone else. But, Jesus let them know that was not what he was talking about.

"So, then Jesus, when the Holy Spirit comes, will it be like it was for our ancestors? When the Spirit came upon Samson, it gave him great strength. It gave him power to defeat the enemy. And do it in style, like the Incredible Hulk or something.'

"Or maybe we will be like Gideon. When the Spirit came upon Gideon, he was transformed from this meek and mild little guy into a champion. Or maybe we will be like any of the other judges and leaders; when the Spirit came upon them, it gave them the strength and power to overcome their enemies and deliver Israel. Will it be that kind of power, Jesus?"

"No," Jesus said, "It won't be like that."

"Okay, so when the Spirit comes on us, he will probably give us the power to live moral lives and keep the law and be just nearly perfect."

"No," Jesus said. "You will receive power to be my witnesses.[35] That is the power you will receive.

I know that doesn't sound like as much fun as being given some superhero power. But the truth is we need power to be witnesses. It is hard to be a witness to the love of Christ. It is hard to be a witness to the will of God. We struggle with these things. We need help. We need power.

We need power because unless we are careful, we end up making it about us. But, in a courtroom, a witness does not talk about herself. She simply tells what she knows about whatever she witnessed. That is our role. We simply tell people what we know about Jesus. We tell people what we have seen God do in our lives and the lives of others. It isn't about my opinion or my thoughts on the matter. It is to tell what we have been able to see God doing. We need power to do that.

Power. I would love to see that power. I don't know about you, but sometimes I am a little saddened by the lack of power I see in the church in general. I don't mean the power to make people act the way we want them to. I don't mean the power to make people stop playing little league sports on Sunday. I don't mean the power to get our way in the culture. I am talking about real power.

I am talking about the power to worship so passionately that our lives are renewed every time we come together to worship God. I am

---

[35] Fred Craddock, *The Collected Sermons of Fred Craddock, pp. 199-200.*

talking about the power to love so genuinely that lives all around us are changed by it. I am talking about the power to put God above every other concern in our lives and live out His kingdom here in this place. "Your will be done on earth as it is in heaven."

Instead of grasping at political power in a way that chases people away, I long to see us have the power of the Holy Spirit that is so honest and loving and authentic that it draws people to God.

There is a story that supposedly occurred back in the day when the church had all kinds of political power and wealth. The Pope was with his assistant. They were going over the wealth of the church, which was quite large. The Pope snickered and said, "I don't guess we can say anymore, like Peter did, 'Gold and Silver have I none.'" His assistant replied. "Neither can we say, 'In the name of Jesus, rise up and walk.'"

Jesus promised that we would receive power. The real kind. The kind that changes our lives and the lives of those around us.

That promise of that power was fulfilled on the Day of Pentecost. The Holy Spirit did come. He entered the lives of the men and the women in the upper room that day. The Holy Spirit came in the form of wind, like the wind that revived the dry bones in the valley in the Book of Ezekiel. The Holy Spirit came in the form of fire, like the fire that led the people of Israel through the desert. The Holy Spirit came in the form of languages and tongues, like the languages that erupted at the tower of Babel, only this time in reverse. At Babel, human speech was confused with different languages so that people could not understand one another. At Pentecost, God used the miracle of languages and speech so everyone could hear and understand the Good News.[36]

They received the power Jesus promised. The power to be witnesses. Over three thousand people became followers of Jesus on that day. The church was born on that day. The path wasn't easy, but the church continued to move forward with the power of the Holy

---

[36] Barbara Brown Taylor, Bread of Angels, p.67.

Spirit. It was a power that helped them to overcome boundaries that were political, racial and economic. It was the Holy Spirit that put the power in their actions and accomplished so much for the Kingdom of God.

Today, when we think of the Holy Spirit, we often think of the presence of God that comforts us and gives us peace when we are going through difficult times. We often think of the Holy Spirit as one who nudges us and guides us in the direction God wants us to go. We often think of the Holy Spirit as the one who helps us understand what the Scripture says and how to apply it to our lives. And the Holy Spirit does all of those things.

But, we often forget the Holy Spirit is more than that. The Holy Spirit is also the wind that blows through our lives with enough force to bend the palm trees over and rip shingles off of the roof. The Holy Spirit is the fire that rages out of control and purifies the junk in our lives. The Holy Spirit is the power that gives us the courage to take risks, to love beyond our comfort zone, and to step out in faith when we aren't so sure about our footing. There is that side of the Holy Spirit as well.

So, the Day of Pentecost is an important reminder for us. I pray that the Holy Spirit, like the wind, would blow strong on us, tearing loose the things in our lives that we need to turn loose. I pray that the Holy Spirit, like fire, would set us ablaze with a passion for God that cannot be quenched. I pray that we would accept not just the promise but also the power of the Holy Spirit of God to be witnesses for God and His kingdom.

We need the power of the Holy Spirit to take us beyond what we can do in our own power. That is where faith takes us. That is where the real living resides.

What I wouldn't give for a power-hungry church. Not the short-lived, measly power of political leverage, but the power of the Holy Spirit. The power to really change lives.

§

Living In the Extraordinary

In the Christian year, there are times of the year designated as Ordinary Time. We seem to think of most of our lives as ordinary time. We live ordinary lives in ordinary times, except for the really hard times (shadows) and really good times (light.)

But, I believe we are wrong when we think this way. There is no such thing as an ordinary day. Every day is a gift. Every day is an opportunity to experience the wonder of life. I believe we live in extraordinary time every day that we open our eyes. Whether that day is filled with good or bad or a mixture of both, it is a gift. We get to experience another day!

These last stories are of people who experienced some of the extraordinary in the midst of what they thought was an ordinary day. I hope the same happens to you. I hope their stories will intersect with your story, and you will see just how extraordinary your life really is.

§

First and Last (Matthew 20: 1-16)

This parable upsets our sense of fairness. We all know that life is not fair, but surely God will be fair.

Surely. God. Will. Be. Fair.

But, in this parable, God doesn't even seem to be fair.

It upsets our assumptions that if we work hard, show up first and leave last, our reward will be greater than those who don't work as hard as we do. Jesus is messing with us here.

The farmer goes out where the day laborers are standing around hoping to get hired, and he picks a few to come and work on his farm. Later, when he goes back into town, some day laborers are still standing around.

"Why are you still standing here? Why aren't you out working?"

"No one hired us. We want to work, but there are no jobs for us."

"Get in," he says. Then he takes them back to his farm and puts them to work.

He goes back into town and sees the same thing. More unemployed people. So, he hires them. Then he does the same thing again and again. The last crew ends up only working for him for an hour or so.

At the end of the day, he tells his foreman to line them up, those hired last at the head of the line, those hired first at the end of the line. Then he paid those hired last a denarius, a fair wage for a day's work. The others who had been working all day, who had agreed to work all day for a denarius, started thinking they would get more. But, when they arrived at the pay station, they received the same amount. They were angry. Most of us read this and are thinking, "I would be too!" I am not sure why the thought of some poor people getting more than we think they deserve bothers some people so much, but it does.

The owner tells them to take their money and go. He paid them a fair wage for a fair day's work. They all agreed on it. If he wants to be generous, that's his business. Then, of course, Jesus ends the story with "The Last shall be first, and the First shall be Last."

There are a lot of ways to look at this story to try to understand it. We can consider its context in the Gospel of Matthew. The story immediately preceding this one in chapter 19 of Matthew's Gospel is the story of Peter, basically asking Jesus, "What's in this for us?"

Peter told Jesus, "We have left everything to follow you. What will there be for us?" We have followed you longer and worked harder than these other folks, so we should get more." Jesus told Peter, "The first will be last, and the last will be first."

Then, immediately following this story, after Jesus predicts his death, James and John's mother wants to know if, when his kingdom becomes reality, Jesus will give her two sons thrones right next to him, one on his right and the other on his left. "Sorry about your impending suffering and death, Jesus, but can you do something for my boys?" Jesus told her the best seats in the house were not his to give.

So, the story falls between two other stories where Jesus' disciples are jockeying for a better position in the kingdom. Since they have given up more, they deserve more. Since they have been there from the beginning, they deserve the best seats. That is how it works in the world they grew up in and in the one we live in. Maybe the story was a reminder to them, and us, that is not how it works in the Kingdom of God.

Imagine how this was received in the congregation reading Matthew's Gospel for the first time. In that new church, there were people there who were Jewish and had followed Jewish laws and customs their whole lives. Sitting next to them were Gentile believers who had never followed any of the Jewish laws. I mean, it didn't seem fair. These Gentiles were church members on the same level as their Jewish counterparts. They had not given up shrimp and bacon their whole lives, yet they were treated the same! Like the thief on the cross who slipped into heaven at the last minute. He didn't have to sacrifice anything, following God for years on end, and he gets the same heaven we do! What about those of us who tithe and go to committee meetings. It's not fair! Deathbed conversions. They get the same mansions in heaven that we do? The same number of bathrooms? It is just not right.

Think for a minute about those who did not get picked. When the farm owner went back out later in the day and saw them still standing there and asked them why they weren't working, they said because no one had picked them to go and work. The text is clear that they have been standing there all day. They had gotten there early in the morning, just like the ones who had gotten picked, but they didn't' get any jobs. They weren't picked.

Ever wonder why they didn't get picked? I'll bet it was for the same reasons people don't get picked today. The younger, stronger men got picked first. I don't know if there were any women out there, but there could have been widowed moms trying to feed their families. But, if there were, they would not have been picked first. The men get picked first. I'll bet if your skin was the wrong color, you didn't get picked first. If you had a foreign accent, you didn't get picked first. If you were too old, you didn't get picked first. If you had any kind of disability, you didn't get picked first.

You see how it works. We create systems that reward those who create the systems and penalize those outside the systems. Then we blame those outside the system and accuse them of being lazy and somehow not as deserving as those of us who are on the inside. We don't pick them and then blame them for not being picked.

The ones who had worked hard all day were watching from the end of the line. They saw those who had not worked as long getting a day's wage for less work. So, they assumed they would be getting paid more than they agreed upon. Surely, if those folks hired at the end of the day got a denarius, they would get more than just one denarius.

After all, these Johnny-come-latelies worked less, and they were the ones that no one else would pick. They should just be happy they have a job. Surely, they won't get paid as much as me. Some of them were old. They didn't work as hard as we did. Some of them were disabled. Some of them didn't even speak Aramaic. Surely, they won't be treated like us. And the women, Lord knows they will only get 72 cents on the denarius that we men get. So, we should get more.

But then he paid them all the same.

The same.

And look at what they said: *"You have made them equal to us!"*

That may be the most telling line in the whole parable. That may be the kicker. "How dare you make *those* people equal to us." We were picked first. They are not the kind you pick first. I don't know, but somewhere in here I feel a sting to our racism, sexism, ageism, xenophobia, and white privilege. If it weren't true we wouldn't have to have laws that try to ensure equal hiring practices, flawed as they are. "You have made them equal to us." Once you do that, it's all over. We lose our power to be first. We have to compete with everyone else on an equal playing field. That is hard to swallow if you have always run downhill. It's hard to give up that advantage.

But, the farm owner says, "Hey, it's my money. I can do what I want with my own money. Are you mad at me because I am generous?"

Darn right they were. It wasn't fair.

You know, it's sort of amazing to me that 99% of us, when we hear this story, we identify with the people who worked all day and got paid the same as those who didn't work all day. We always identify with the ones who we think got ripped off. That is why this parable disturbs us so. Because we identify with those who should have been first but ended up last.

We don't often identify with the ones who were picked last. The ones who got up early and went to the town square, but no one picked them to work for them. We never identify with the ones who skirted in on the last few hours of work and got the same amount of money as those who worked all day. So, we say the parable isn't fair.

But, the news that everyone is getting paid the same sounds very different, depending on where you are standing in line. If you are at the back of the line, expecting to get more, then it is bad news. It is unfair.

But, if you are at the front of the line, and realize that not only did you get put at the front of the line, but you are going to get paid more than you deserve, then it is Good News. You are getting more than you deserve. It's not fair, but no one is going to complain about that. From the back of the line, it sounds unfair. It is terrible news. But, from the front of the line, it sounds great. It is Good News. If you are used to being First, it is bad news. But, if you are used to being Last, this is Good News.

Compared to the early disciples, the martyrs, and many others, maybe we didn't get to work as early as we think we did. Maybe, compared to what others have sacrificed for God, we really aren't the first ones in the field. Maybe, in the end, we get paid more than we are worth; we are given more than we deserve. Not because of who we are, but because of who God is[37].

Here's the truth. God is not fair. God is generous. That's the Good News. That is Good News for all of us.

§

---

[37] Barbara Brown Taylor, The Seeds of Heaven, "Beginning at the End," p.106.

God and The Empire (Matthew 22:15-22)

It seems that wherever Jesus went these days, there was a crowd of people. Many came to hear what he had to say and maybe catch a miracle or two. Some were earnestly seeking whether or not he was the promised Messiah. And then, there were the Pharisees and Herodians. They came to try to trip up Jesus, get him to say something he shouldn't. If they couldn't get him into trouble with the authorities, they hoped to at least embarrass him. The Pharisees and Herodians were strange bedfellows. But, you do what you have to do.

They begin by flattering Jesus.

"Jesus, we know that you are a man of integrity. You always shoot straight, and you are bi-partisan."

Then they did what they came for. They asked a loaded question, "Is it right to pay the imperial tax to Caesar, or not?" It was a trick question because Jesus would be in trouble either way he answered, or so they thought.

If Jesus said, "Get yourself a good tax attorney and don't pay any taxes to Rome," then they would report him to Pilate and accuse him of anti-Roman activity. Not paying taxes to Rome was not taken lightly.

But, on the other hand, if he said that he supported paying the tax, they believed he would lose some support among his followers because who likes paying taxes, especially paying taxes to an occupying government.

One of the things I admire about Jesus is how he never takes the bait. They gave him two options. He chose neither. Because neither represented who he was. Neither represented the truth of the matter. I wish we were better at that.

Jesus knew what they were up to. He knew their intentions. His reply, *"You hypocrites, why are you trying to trap me? Show me the coin used for paying the tax."*

Apparently, Jesus didn't have a coin in his pockets, so one of his accusers had to cough up one. On the front of the coin was an image of the head of Caesar Tiberius or the Emperor Tiberius, similar to some of our coins that have the image of Lincoln or Washington on them. The inscription read, "Tiberius Caesar, son of Divine Augustus." On the back of the coin was the image of a woman. Some scholars say it is supposed to be the image of his mother. Others say it is the personification of peace. Some say it's both.

They handed it to Jesus. He looked at it, turned it over in his hand, then answered their question with a question.

"Whose image is this? And whose inscription?"

"Caesar." They replied.

"So, give back to Caesar what is Caesar's, and to God what is God's."

His answer left them with their chins on the floor. They didn't know what to say. Not only did he avoid their trap and not choose between the lesser of two evils, but he spoke a truth that left them and us wondering about the full application of what he said.

Give to Caesar what is Caesar's and to God what is God's. That has always been a tricky issue. Give to the Empire what is the Empire's and to God what is God's. Give to the United States of America what is the USA's and give to God what is God's. What belongs to the government and what belongs to God?

Remember the inscription on that coin?

"Tiberius Caesar, son of the Divine Augustus. Romans believed their leaders were not only god-ordained but were Divine themselves. They believed that Caesar—every Caesar—was a god.

We often neglect this setting in which Jesus lived and taught. But, it had significant influence over many of the things Jesus said and did. It is also the reason he was crucified and his followers persecuted for decades. Following the Empire and following Jesus were not the same thing. They never are.

Here are some of Caesar's titles found in writings and inscriptions on monuments during New Testament times and before.

"Caesar is Lord."

That is how people in the Roman Empire referred to Caesar. Caesar is Lord. Did you realize that when Paul used the phrase "Jesus is Lord," it was not only confessional; It was subversive. In the first century, when Christians were baptized, their confession of faith was, "Jesus is Lord." And that confession could get you into trouble. It was more than a religious statement. It was a political statement. Who is your Lord? Caesar or Jesus.

"Prince of Peace."

Because of the Pax Romana, the peace through violence campaign of the Roman Empire, Caesar was given the title, "Prince of Peace." There was peace because no one wanted to get crucified or fed to the lions. There was peace because people were too afraid to stand up to the Roman government until they weren't. It didn't last. To say that Jesus is the Prince of Peace was to claim that the way of peace is not through violence, but thorough justice, love, and nonviolence, the way that Jesus taught.

"Savior of the World."

The Romans were busy colonizing the known world and, in their view, trying to make it more civilized, more Roman. They made people behave like the Romans thought they should behave. Therefore, they were saving the world, and Caesar was the savior of the world. When we call Jesus savior of the world, we mean something completely different. We mean the one who came and gave his own life to offer us forgiveness. He came to save us from ourselves and make us not like the Romans but like God created us to be.

I find it telling that Jesus asked, "Whose image is on the coin?"

Caesar's image was on the coin. Since Caesar's image was on the coin, give the coin back to him. It's his. It has his image on it. The

Bible says that you and I were created in the image of God. We have God's image on us. If someone looks at you and asks, "Whose image is in that person?" The answer is God's. You are made in God's image, so you belong to God.

Give to Caesar what is Caesar's and to God what is God's. There has always been conflict between Caesar and God, between empires and God, between governments and God. Let me illustrate this for us today.

When we decide how we are going to treat our neighbor, who guides us in that decision? Wear a mask, or don't wear a mask. Bring them food, or don't bring them food. Help them while they are without a job, or don't help them. Who guides our thinking on these issues? Is Caesar Lord, or is Jesus Lord?

When it comes to peace, how do we think it will be achieved. Will peace come because we bring in more troops and treat people who don't comply with our rules with violence? Will we rain down enough violence to keep everyone in line? Or will we work for justice, see that everyone is treated equally and justly? Peace through violence or peace through justice? Who is our Prince of Peace? Is it Caesar, or is it Jesus?

Who is our savior? Who will save us from the things we fear? Just like the Caesars, governments and politicians have always promised to be our savior. They claim to be the only ones who can save us from our enemies and from people who are not like us. They will save us through military and political power.

Or, do we trust that the one who died on the cross, who offers us a much harder path to follow, is the only one who can save us? Save us, not just from our enemies, but also from our own sin? Who is our savior? Is it Caesar, or is it Jesus?

For most of history, it has been impossible to be a good patriot and be a good Christian, simply because government goals and methods do not line up with the goals and methods of Jesus. When we make any nation, any political party, any candidate the same as God or God's kingdom, then we have done exactly what Jesus warned us against. We have given to Caesar what is God's. Some call it Nationalism. The Bible calls it idolatry.

I love this nation, but I love Jesus more. My citizenship in this country is second to my citizenship in the Kingdom of God. You hear how subversive that sounds to those who want government and country to be your first allegiance? Patriotism is too small for the God who created every nationality and tribe and every person on earth.

I like the way Will Willimon put it when he wrote,

> "Perhaps the best we can hope, in matters between Christians and the state, is to be permanently uneasy, always willing to be surprised by the range of Christ's Lordship, always willing to obey God rather than human authority."[38]

The conflict is real. Who will we trust to be the Lord of our lives? Who will we trust to be our Prince of Peace? Who will we trust to be our Savior?

Give to Caesar what is Caesar's and to God what is God's.

§

---

[38] *Will Willimon, Lectionary Sermon Resource, Year A, Part 2, p.219.*

The Preacher and The Pretty Woman
(The Book of Hosea)

The story of Hosea is one of my favorite stories from the Hebrew Bible. First of all, let me say there are a lot of different interpretations concerning exactly what happened between Hosea and his wife, Gomer. The information is skimpy, and you have to read between the lines to put the story together. So, I am going to tell you the story the way I believe it happened.

Hosea was a fundamentalist preacher. He was a prophet. He was convinced the nation was going to hell in a handbasket. He stood on the street corner with a bullhorn telling people to "Repent." "Turn or burn!" He wore a sandwich sign that said, "Judgement is Coming" on one side, and on the other side it said, "Hell is Hot." Part of the job description of a prophet is to denounce things, and Hosea was good at it. He denounced everything and everybody. Denouncing can make you feel sort of powerful, but it does not get you many invitations to parties.

Gomer was nearly the complete opposite of Hosea. She had a hard life. She grew up in a rough home. She wore too much make-up, and her skirts were a little short. Gomer didn't denounce sin; she rather enjoyed it. She had a reputation for being a "fun" date.

Somehow Hosea and Gomer fell in love. Nobody understood what they saw in each other. They say opposites attract. They were certainly opposites, and they were attracted to one another. They were quite a pair; a strait-laced preacher and a satin and lace party girl. To everyone's surprise they got married. I would have loved to have attended the reception. I would have loved to have been there to watch her friends and family and his friends and family mingling around the punch bowl. That had to be interesting!

About ten months into the marriage, they had their first child, a son. When it came to giving him a name, Hosea was firm. They named him Jezreel. Jezreel was the well-known name of a place where there was a massacre, and it became a symbol of government corruption. If you mention the word Jezreel, people would just start shaking their heads and agree on how corrupt the government had gotten. It would sort of be like naming your first-born child "Water-gate."[39] Every time the teacher called his son's name at school, Hosea scored a point in absentia.

Later, their second child was born. This child was a little girl. Hosea insisted she be named Lo-ruhamah, which means "not loved." What a terrible thing to do to a child. What a terrible name. Life is hard enough without giving someone a name like that. Many scholars suspect the double meaning in the name was that Hosea wasn't sure she was his child. At any rate, it is a horrible name to get stuck with. You can only hope her friends just called her "Lo."

Soon afterward, the third child was born. Any resemblance between this child and Hosea was purely coincidental. Hosea named this one "not mine." That pretty much tells you everything you need to know.

By this point, Hosea's relationship with Gomer had become quite rocky. We aren't given any details about when or how, but one day Gomer just up and left. She "R-u-n-n O-f-t." She decided that she did not want to be tied down anymore to this old-fashioned Bible thumper and three preschoolers. She had had enough Bible studies and diapers. So, she packed her bags and left Hosea a note telling him he could color her gone. He could pick up the kids at her mother's.

Hosea got home, found the note, then went and got the kids. Hosea found himself abandoned. He was a single parent before any-

---

[39] *Stephen Shoemaker, Retelling the Biblical Story, p.84.*

one had even coined the term. He was left with three preschoolers, and two of them weren't even his. I try to imagine the next part of the story. I know this story is, unfortunately, a reality for a lot of people.

Hosea preached and denounced all day, then picked up the kids from daycare and went home. He fed them supper, gave them baths, read them stories, and put them to bed. Then, I imagine it happened something like this. After the kids were asleep, Hosea sat alone in his bedroom with the lights out. He thought about his life. About how things had not turned out the way he had planned. He thought about how Gomer, the only woman he had ever loved, had rejected him. He prayed, and he started crying.

He said out loud, "God, why me?" "I have tried to do everything you have asked me to do. I stand on the street corner, yelling like a fool. People spit at me and make fun of me. And now, the one person I loved the most has left me. God, you have no idea how bad this hurts. You have no idea what it is like to be abandoned by someone you love more than anything else in the world."

Then, God spoke to Hosea some of the most powerful words in the Hebrew Bible. God said, "Hosea, I know exactly how you feel. I have loved Israel with all of my heart, and they have been unfaithful to me. They have abandoned me. I know exactly how you feel." With those words, we are reminded not only how much God loved Israel but how much God loves us.

Hosea said, "Well, God, what are we going to do? The people you love have been unfaithful and have left you. The woman I love has been unfaithful and left me. So, what do we do now?"

God said, "Well, I am going to win her back. I am going to allure her. I will speak tenderly to her and win her back. The day will come when she will call me, 'my husband' and no longer 'my master.'" These are not words of religion. These are words of romance. God is so in love with Israel that even after she has been unfaithful and broken God's heart, God is going to woo her back. Charles Wesley wrote a beautiful hymn that expresses this thought; Jesus Lover Of My Soul. You see, when we sin, we don't break some unseen cosmic law somewhere. We break each other's heart. We break God's heart. And even though we break God's heart, God never stops loving us. We turn God's joyous love for us, like that of a wedding, into a suffering love, like that we see of Jesus suffering on a cross.

"I am going to go win her back, Hosea. Why don't you do the same?"

Hosea went and found Gomer. Things had not worked out so well for her. When Hosea found her, she was working as a prostitute in the temple of Baal. Baal was a Canaanite fertility god. Part of their rituals included prostitution. Just like in our day, there were people in the culture who worshiped sex.

They sacrificed raisin cakes to Baal. A quick word about the raisin cakes. The Israelites had turned to other gods and loved the sacred raisin cakes. Raisin cakes were a part of the offering they would bring to Baal. So, the sin was that they were offering something to a false god. I want to make it absolutely clear that there is nothing wrong with eating raisin cakes! It is not a sin to eat raisin cakes. I don't want anyone reading this thinking that Little Debbie is the anti-Christ or anything like that. This is how rumors get started.

The Baal priests at the temple would not let Hosea take her home unless he bought out her contract. It was fifteen shekels of silver and a homer and a half of barley. It is interesting to note that fifteen shekels of silver was only half the price of a common slave. They sold her back to Hosea for half price. She was damaged goods. They didn't even want her anymore.

I can't imagine how surprised she must have been when the door opened, and it was Hosea. Again, I don't know exactly how it happened, but in my imagination, it went something like this:

Hosea opened the door, she looked up at him, and he smiled and said, "I have always loved you. Nothing you can ever do will make me stop loving you. I have paid the price for your freedom. Come with me. Let's go home." Gomer got up, took him by the hand, and they went home.

I like to think that when they got back home that Gomer changed. I like to think that she learned to love Hosea and became a good wife. I like to think that she learned to love her children and became a good mother.

I think this whole experience changed Hosea too. He threw away the bullhorn and tore up the old signs that said, "Judgement is Coming" and "Hell is Hot," and made a new one. The new sign just said, "God loves You!" It was a small town, so everyone knew their story. Some evenings you would see them strolling together down the sidewalk, holding hands, and when you did, there wasn't a dry eye in the house.[40]

What a beautiful story. What a beautiful love story! But then, it gets even better. Because the Bible says it is not just the story of Hosea and Gomer, but it is also the story of God and us. You see, God loves us and creates us so that we can live in relationship with God.

But, somewhere along the way, we start to think that we know what is best for us. We don't like God's way of doing things. Following God seems boring, so we decide to have some fun and do things our own way. We turn our backs on God and do what we want to do.

Then one day, Jesus finds a way to show up in our lives. And he says to us, "I have always loved you. Nothing you can ever do will make me stop loving you. I have paid the price for your freedom. Follow me. Let's go home."

For the life of me, I don't know how anyone can do anything else but follow him.

§

---

[40] Frederick Buechner, *Peculiar Treasures*, "Gomer" pp.43-44.

The Day A Camel Slipped Through The Eye Of A Needle[41]
(Luke 19: 1-10)

Nobody really knows what was going through Zacchaeus' mind that morning when he got out of bed. It started off like most other mornings. He pulled back the sheets, slid out from under them, then sat on the edge of the bed. His feet did not touch the floor. He slid off of the bed and stumbled across expensive tile and up on a step stool to look in the mirror. His eyes were bloodshot from another night of drinking alone. Over to a walk-in closet the size of most people's houses. He thumbed his way through a row of Armani suits like flipping through a Rolodex (For those of you who remember what a Rolodex was.) After getting dressed, he gave the day's instructions to his household staff and headed for the city. But not to work. Not today. He had other plans.

To help us understand the story, the Bible tells us that Zacchaeus was a chief tax collector. Remember that tax collectors were hated by their fellow Jews. It was a profession that was filled with corruption. Zacchaeus was an Israelite who collected taxes from his own people for the hated Roman government. Not only was he sleeping with the enemy, but he was getting rich doing it. Any money he could collect above what the Romans required from him, he got to keep. So, he extracted as much money as he could from his neighbors and kinsman.

And Zacchaeus wasn't just a tax collector. He was a Chief Tax Collector. That means he had other tax collectors working for him, and

---

[41] *Stephen Shoemaker, Retelling the Biblical Story, p.133. The idea for this title comes from here.*

he was getting a cut of their profits too. One didn't get that high in the system by worrying about business ethics.

Jericho was a well-known trade center which made it one of the richest taxation centers in Palestine. Zacchaeus was in the right place, working a corrupt system to his advantage. He was rich, and he was hated.

When I read a story in the Bible, I try to picture it in my mind. Imagine how it happened. If I were making a movie, I would cast Danny DeVito in the role of Zacchaeus. I think he would be a perfect Zacchaeus. Remember the character he played on "Taxi"? Remember Louie? The short, self-centered, cruel, nasty, amoral manager of the cab station. I think Zacchaeus was a lot like Louie. Imagine Jesus and Louie, except in this story Louie is very rich.

Zacchaeus had heard that Jesus was coming through Jericho, so instead of going to the office, he went to the main street to see him. When Zacchaeus arrived, the crowds had already lined both sides of the street. Being vertically impaired, he could not see over the crowd, and there wasn't a chance anyone was going to let him through. Further down the street, he saw a tree next to the road. So, he ran to the tree and climbed it so he could see Jesus when he passed by. That is all he wanted, just a glimpse, just to get a look at the man he had heard so many incredible things about.

Soon, Jesus came down the road with his entourage. The crowd lining the street was so excited. People were cheering, whispering to each other, pointing. They had heard so much about this man who could heal the sick and raise the dead. Everyone wanted to see him. Even Zacchaeus.

When Jesus approached the tree where Zacchaeus was sitting, a surprising thing happened. Jesus stopped and looked up at Zacchaeus. I imagine the crowd got quiet. They didn't want to miss this. I mean, this was Jesus, the most ethical, righteous man any of them had ever heard about, and he was face to face with Zacchaeus. The Son of God is about to say something to Zacchaeus, aka, scum in an expensive suit. They just knew Jesus was going to let him have it. You know Jesus has had some pretty harsh things to say to rich people. Especially those who got rich by exploiting others.

Just a chapter ago, Jesus met a rich young ruler who wanted to follow him. He asked Jesus what he must do. Jesus told him to give away all that he had. The rich man could not do that. He walked away. Jesus turned to his disciples and said,

> *"How hard it is for the rich to enter the kingdom of God. Indeed, it is easier for a camel to go through the eye of a needle than for someone who is rich to enter the kingdom of God."*
>
> Luke 18:25

Oh, boy! Zacchaeus is about to get it. Jesus is going to give it to him.

I am sure Zacchaeus thought he was going to get it too. After all, he deserved it. He knew he was a crook, despite all of the ways he justified to himself what he did. The same way we try to justify things we know are wrong. He just tightened his grip on the tree limb and braced himself. When you are the town sleazeball, the last person you care to have a public conversation with is the visiting evangelist! He knew he was about to get it, so he closed his eyes and braced for the worse. There is no way this is going to end well.

Jesus looked up at him, and I believe he smiled when he said, *"Zacchaeus, come down. I want to have lunch with you today."* The Bible doesn't say how he got down. Frederick Buechner is probably right when he writes that "the chances are good that he fell out in pure astonishment."[42] Chins hit the dirt. People couldn't believe it. They were shocked. They were offended. Then, Jesus and Zacchaeus went off together to lunch. One just down from a tree, the other about to be nailed to a tree.[43]

---

[42] *Frederick Buechner, Wishful Thinking, p.100.*
[43] *Shoemaker, p. 136.*

They went to Zacchaeus' house and had lunch. While they were eating, Zacchaeus stood up and said, *"Look, Lord! Here and now I give half of my possessions to the poor, and if I have cheated anybody out of anything, I will pay back four times the amount."*

Unlike the rich young ruler who could not give up his wealth when Jesus asked, Zacchaeus is willing to give up his wealth without even being asked. Will Willimon points out that Zacchaeus really understood salvation. You can tell because he didn't say, "Wonderful, now I will go to heaven when I die." Instead, he said, "I am going to give what I have on behalf of the poor and make a difference in this world now."[44] That's salvation!

I must confess, this may be my favorite story in all of the Bible. I love the story of Zacchaeus/Louie and Jesus. It is a surprising story. Luke is usually pretty hard on rich people in his Gospel. The reason, I think, is because the more we have, the more self-sufficient we become. The more self-sufficient we are, the harder it is for us to admit that we need God. If we can buy a little happiness here and there, we forget that lasting joy comes only from God. The nice house and the new car can hide the shambles of our relationships and the hurts we carry deep inside. People who think they are self-made tend to worship their creator.

Jesus didn't really say a lot to Zacchaeus about his life and his relationship with God. He didn't have to. The fact that Jesus would invite himself to Zacchaeus' house for lunch said it all. God loved Zacchaeus. He finally got it. He sat there at the end of a long, expensive table for a while. His eyes were watering. Then he announced, "I have something to say."

Jesus smiled and said, "Great Zacchaeus. Stand up and tell us."

Zacchaeus said, "I am standing!"

Then, he announced his changed life and his intentions to give away his wealth to the poor and those he had cheated. His household staff probably fainted. Walter Rauschenbusch commented, "Here a

---

[44] *Will Willimon, Lectionary Sermon Resource, Year C, Part 2, "How Tall Was Jesus," p.211.*

camel passed through the needle's eye, and Jesus stood and cheered."[45]

Occasionally something shakes our self-sufficiency, and we see our need for God. Usually, the thing that shakes us the hardest is God's incredible grace. Someday, somehow, we understand that when God looks at us, God doesn't see just what we have become. God sees what he created us to be. God sees less of what the world has made us and more of how he made us. God sees our sin. But, God also sees our pain and self-doubt, and brokenness. God sees what we have it in us to be, and if we spend enough time with God, by his grace, he draws it out of us. Everyone else looked at Zacchaeus and saw a nasty, cruel, self-centered jerk. Jesus saw a man who could be generous and fair and kind. In the end, look who was right.

The story of Zacchaeus is the Bible in a nutshell. It is a story about our sinfulness and bravado and God's relentless love. It is a story about how one day we decide to go looking for God and find out God was looking for us the whole time. And when we encounter God, our lives are changed, and we find life like we had only dreamed of before.

It really happened one day a long time ago. It wasn't a magic trick. It wasn't an illusion. A camel slipped through the eye of a needle. A self-sufficient man realized his need for God and found new life. What about you? You may not consider yourself rich, but have you lived a self-sufficient life for so long that you don't know how to give God a chance? You have substituted your own best for God's best for you. And there is no real comparison. When you are willing to lay aside your self-sufficiency and trust your life to God, you will find God is waiting to receive you. Once again, the camel will pass through the eye of the needle. And, once again, Jesus will stand and cheer!

---

[45] *Walter Rauschenbusch, Quoted by Stephen Shoemaker, ibid. p. 136.*

CPSIA information can be obtained
at www.ICGtesting.com
Printed in the USA
LVHW030918130522
718694LV00010B/801